VOLUME II

The Development
of Western Music

AN ANTHOLOGY

Charles M. Atkinson

VOLUME II

The Development
of Western Music

AN ANTHOLOGY

Pre-Classical, Classical, Romantic

Edited by

K Marie Stolba

Professor of Music
Indiana University-Purdue University at Fort Wayne

Wm. C. Brown Publishers

Book Team

Editor *Meredith M. Morgan*
Developmental Editor *Dean Robbins*
Production Editor *Diane Clemens*
Designer *David C. Lansdon*
Permissions Editor *Vicki Krug*

 Wm. C. Brown Publishers

President *G. Franklin Lewis*
Vice President, Publisher *George Wm. Bergquist*
Vice President, Publisher *Thomas E. Doran*
Vice President, Operations and Production *Beverly Kolz*
National Sales Manager *Virginia S. Moffat*
Senior Marketing Manager *Kathy Law Laube*
Marketing Manager *Kathleen Nietzke*
Managing Editor, Production *Colleen A. Yonda*
Production Editorial Manager *Julie A. Kennedy*
Production Editorial Manager *Ann Fuerste*
Publishing Services Manager *Karen J. Slaght*
Manager of Visuals and Design *Faye M. Schilling*

Cover illustration by Alex Boies

Copyright © 1991 by Wm. C. Brown Publishers. All rights reserved

Library of Congress Catalog Card Number: 90–55352

ISBN 0–697–01135–6

Printed in the United States of America by Wm. C. Brown Publishers,
2460 Kerper Boulevard, Dubuque, IA 52001

10 9 8 7 6 5 4 3 2 1

S. D. G.

Contents

Preface   ix

Preface

The Development of Western Music: An Anthology is a historical anthology of music specifically designed to present music to be studied in conjunction with the text *The Development of Western Music: A History*. The Anthology was originally conceived as a two-volume presentation of representative music. However, when it became apparent that, because of the length of many nineteenth-century compositions, Volume II would probably be unwieldy, the decision was made to produce a three-volume set. Volume I comprises music from Ancient, Medieval, Renaissance, and Baroque eras; Volume II holds Pre-Classical, Classical, and Romantic works; and Volume III contains selections from the Late Nineteenth Century and Twentieth Century. With few exceptions, the selections are complete movements or complete compositions. The works are presented in the Anthology in the same order in which they are mentioned or discussed in the History text. Most of the selections in the Anthology have been recorded, and many of the selections are included in two boxed sets of recordings that are available in LP, CD, or cassette form for use with the Anthology and the History. The music is printed in the Anthology in its original key; however, the recording, particularly of vocal music, may be in a different key.

Texts of vocal music are presented in their original language, with English translation. Most of the translations of poetic and prose texts are my own; the work of other persons is acknowledged. I am indebted to Father Dick John of St. Francis College, Fort Wayne, for assistance with some medieval Latin, especially those texts containing particular ecclesiastical expressions, and to Miguel Roig-Francoli for help in translating some Spanish and Galician poetry.

Although this Anthology was designed to complement the History text, the Anthology is complete in itself, and its selections can serve as works for study and analysis in Form and Analysis, Music Theory, or other music courses.

It is impossible to name all those who contributed to this project. From time to time, several of my colleagues, particularly, John Loessi and Masson Robertson, have loaned me music from their personal libraries. Jody Smith graciously consented to copy into music calligraphy my transcriptions from manuscripts. Many libraries have shared their holdings with me. Great demands have been made upon the Music Library at Indiana University, Bloomington, and thanks are due especially to Music Librarians R. Michael Fling and Cathy Talalay, and their reference assistants Julie Schnepel and Miguel Roig-Francoli, all of whom responded promptly to my numerous requests for materials. The librarians in the Inter-Library Loan/Document Delivery Services department at Helmke Library, IPFW, were most helpful in procuring materials. Marilyn Grush spent many hours with me researching sources at the OCLC station there. I wish to express my gratitude to Kenneth Balthaser, who made available the facilities at the IPFW Learning Resource Center and the services of its technicians in the preparation of camera-ready proof, particularly, Roberta Shadle and James Whitcraft.

Where no specific modern publication is cited, the music was transcribed and/or edited from original sources. Wm. C. Brown Publishers and I are grateful to the persons and publishers who have granted permission to reprint, edit, or adapt material for which they hold copyright. I wish to express my appreciation also to my editors at Wm. C. Brown Publishers, who carefully considered my requests, and to my book team and all other persons who were involved in the production of these volumes.

K Marie Stolba
Fort Wayne, Indiana

139. MONTEZUMA, Aria di Erissena: "Godi l'amabile"
Karl H. Graun (1703/4-1759)

Godi l'amabile presente istante
ch' è il vero ed unico ben della vita;

dal timor libera, amo il tuo amante,
l'impresa seguita a cui t'invita
un dolce e tenero, un dolce e tenero,
  soave amor.

Enjoy the charming present moment
which is the true and only happiness of
  life;
free from fear, love your beloved,
pursue the undertaking to which
a sweet and tender, a sweet and tender,
  gentle love invites you.

140. SONATA IN D MAJOR, K. 119 (Longo 415)
Domenico Scarlatti (1685-1757)

141. SYMPHONY NO. 3, in F Major, H. 665 (W. 183)
C. P. E. Bach (1714–1788)

Breitkopf & Härtel, Wiesbaden
Only the first movement is on the record set.

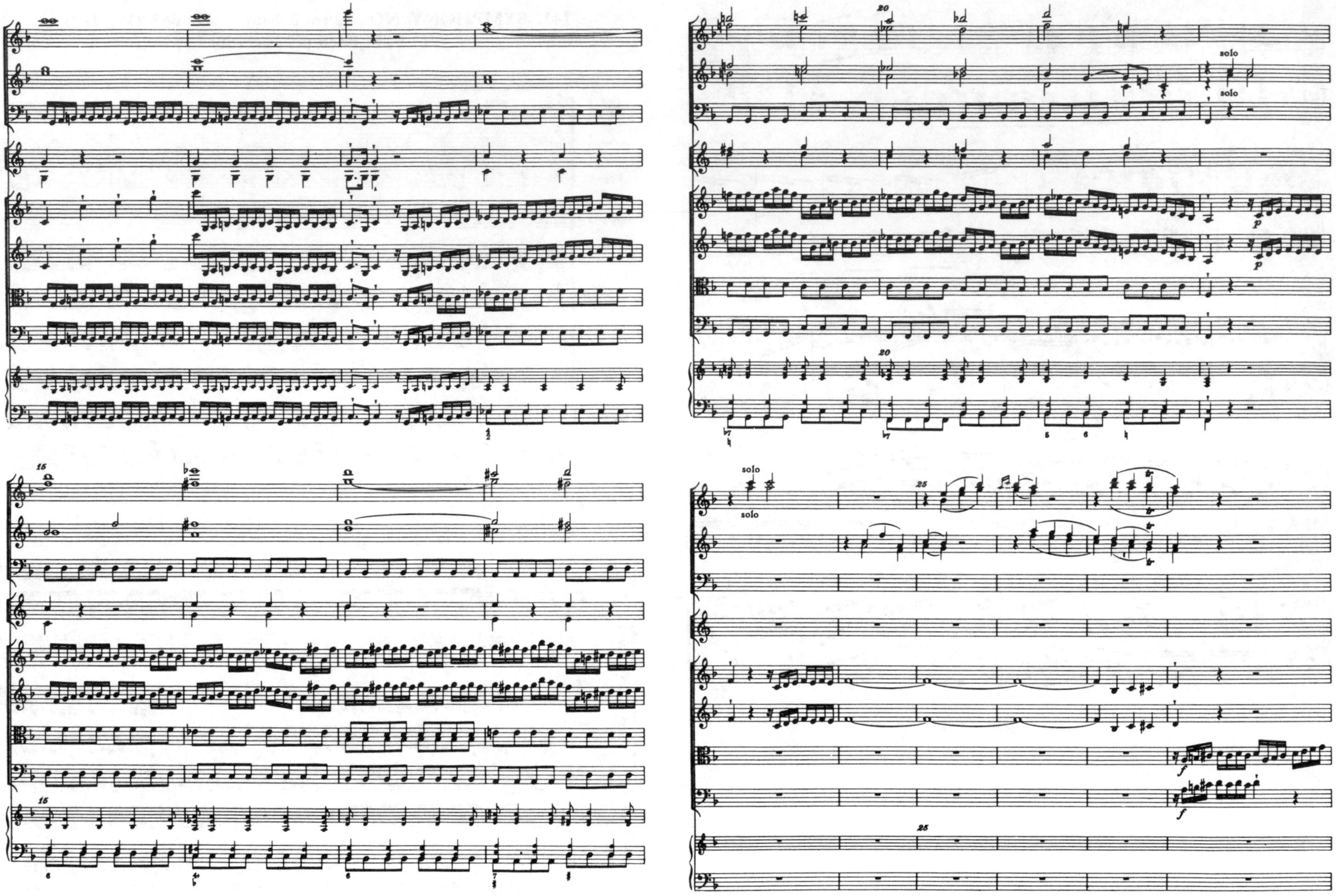
solo
solo
solo
solo

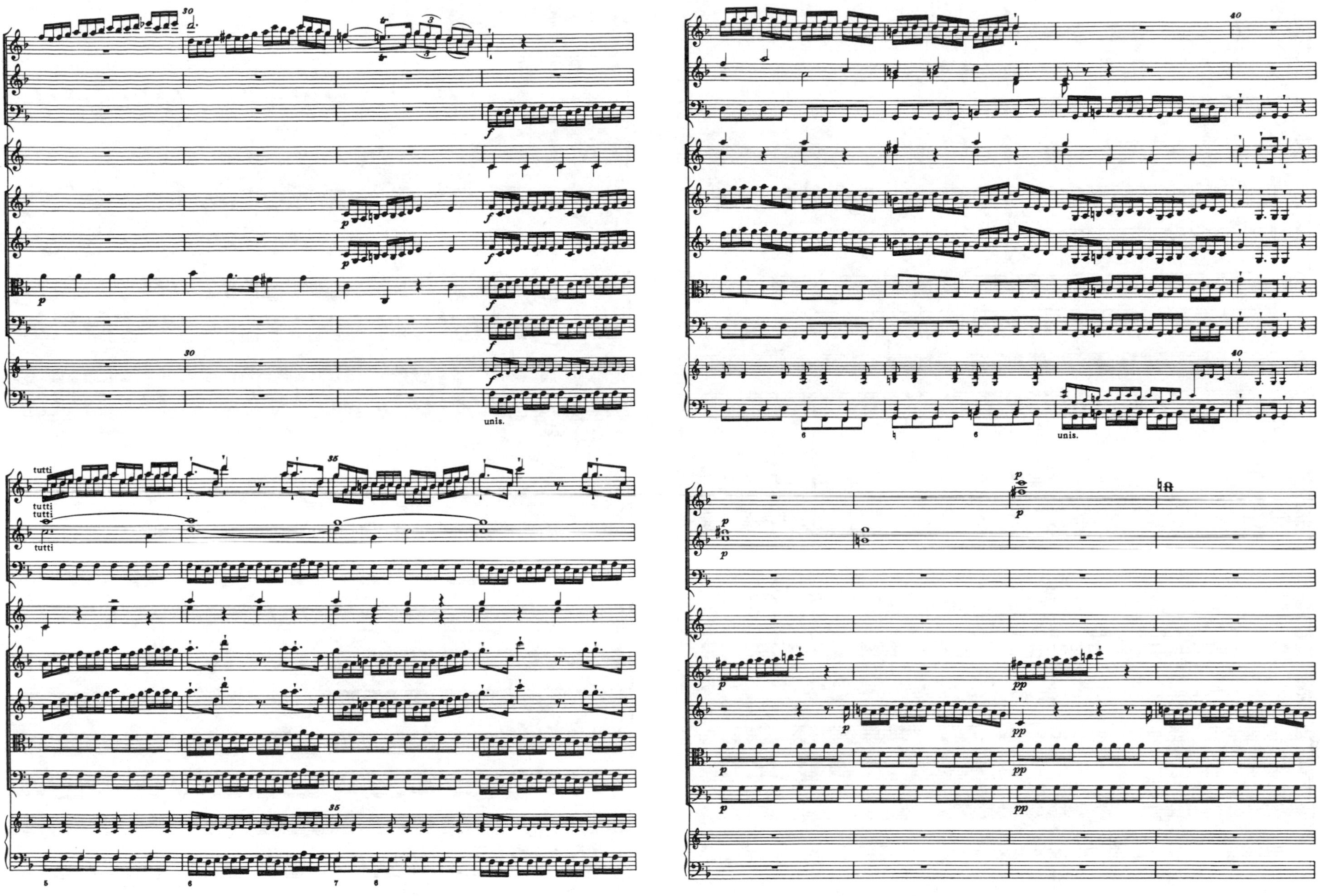
unis.
tutti
tutti
tutti
tutti
unis.

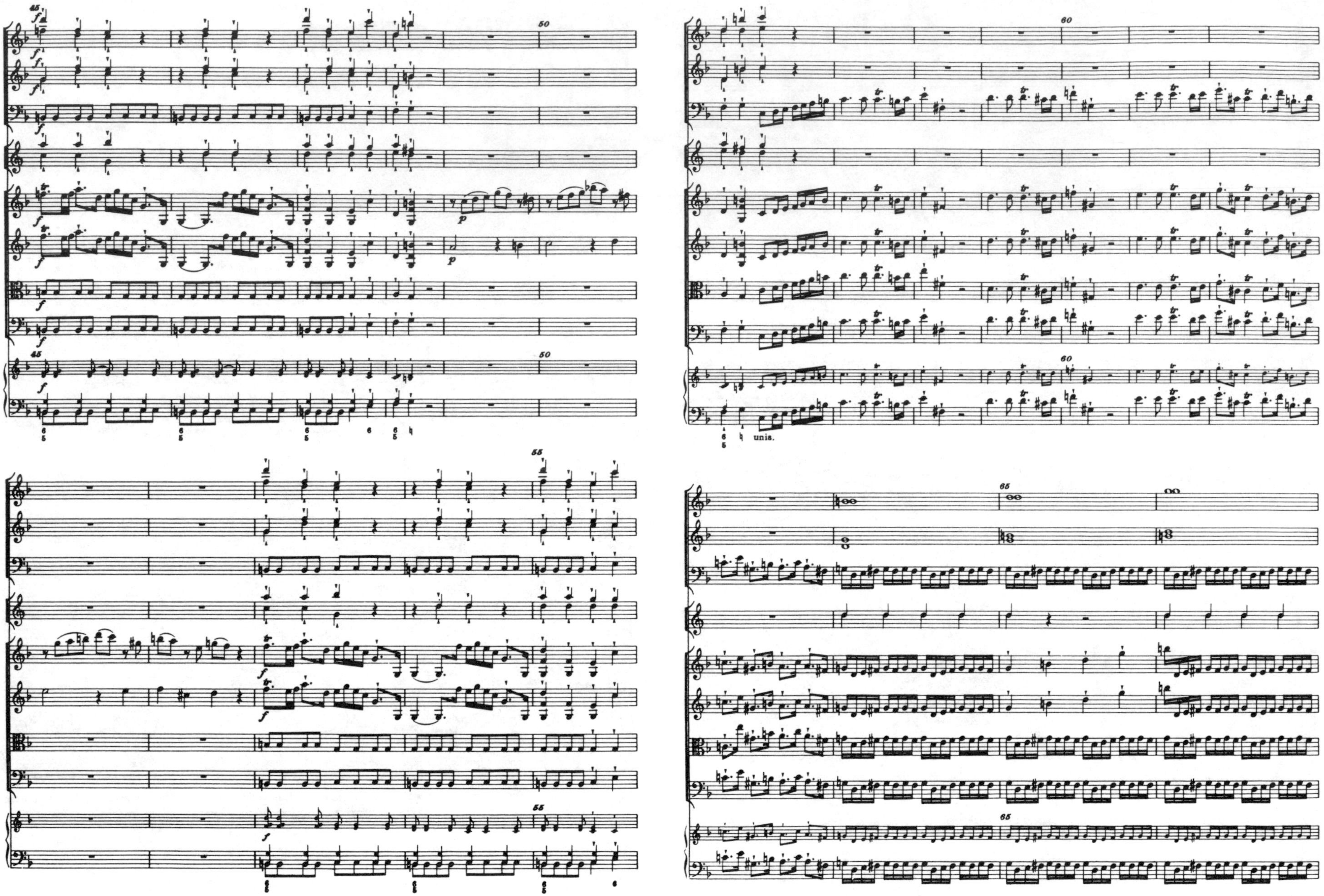
unis.

142. SYMPHONY NO. 32, in F Major
Giovanni Battista Sammartini (1701-1775)

I

Reprinted by permission of the publishers from *The Thematic Catalog of the Works of Giovanni Battista Sammartini*, edited by Newell Jenkins and Bathia Churgin, Cambridge, Mass.: Harvard University Press, Copyright © 1968 by the President and Fellows of Harvard College.

Only the first movement is on the record set.

*m. 35: In mm. 35-36, the octave skips in the manuscript are reversed, starting with the upper octave and descending.

II

Andante

* m. 6: ♫♫ in vn. II. However, the rhythmic differentiation of the cadence here and in m. 36 seems to be deliberate and should be preserved.

III

*mm. 55, 58: *bb* tied over in the manuscript.

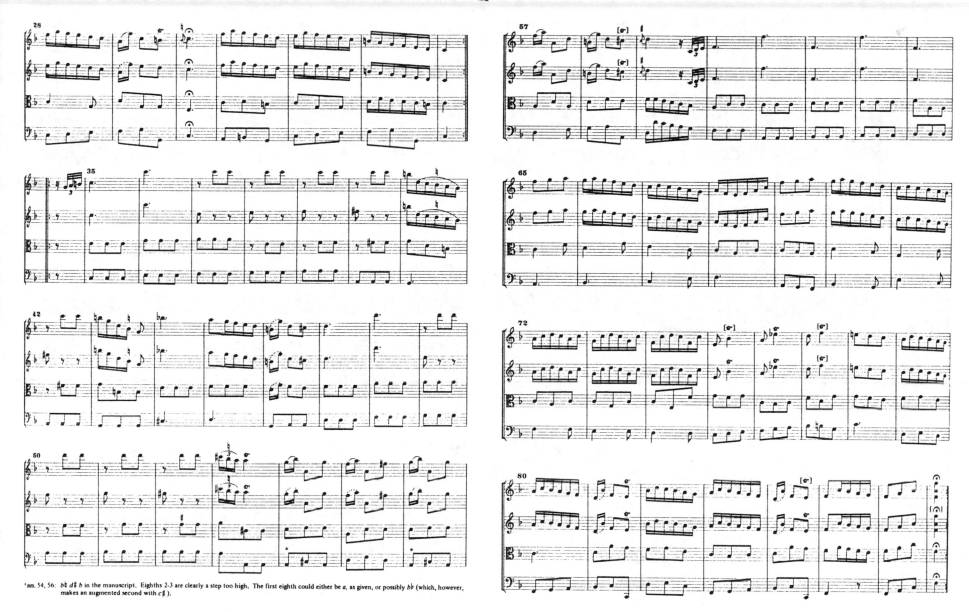

'mm. 54, 56: *b♭ d♯ b* in the manuscript. Eighths 2-3 are clearly a step too high. The first eighth could either be *a*, as given, or possibly *b♭* (which, however, makes an augmented second with *c♯*).

143. SINFONIA A 8, No. 1, in D Major, mvt. 1
Johann Václav Anton Stamitz (1717-1757)

Source: Breitkopf & Härtel, Leipzig, 1902.

N.B. The small notes are variants in the Paris edition.

24

144. L'OLIMPIADE, Act II, Aria: "Se cerca, se dice"
Giovanni Battista Pergolesi (1710–1736)

Source: Harvard University Press, Cambridge, MA

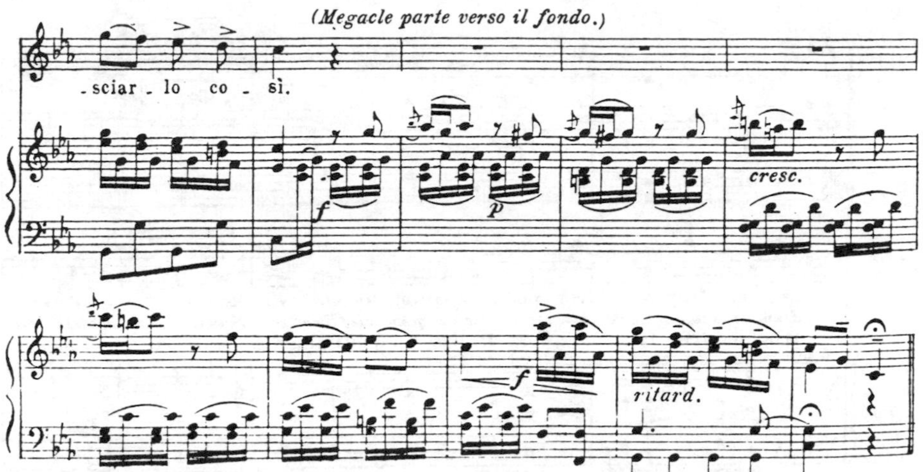
(Megacle parte verso il fondo.)
-sciar - lo co - sì.
cresc.
ritard.

Se cerca, se dice:
l'amico dov'è?
l'amico infelice, (rispondi), mori:
Ah, no! Sì gran duolo non darle
per me . . .
Rispondi, ma solo: piangendo partì.
Che abisso di pene lasciare il suo bene,

lasciarlo per sempre, lasciarlo così!

If she seeks, if she says:
"Where is my lover?"
Reply: "The unfortunate lover died."
Ah, no! Do not give her such great
sorrow for me . . .
Reply, only: "He went away weeping."
What an abyss of distress to leave one's
love,
to leave it for ever, to leave it thus!

145. LA SERVA PADRONA, Duetto: "Lo conosco"
Giovanni Battista Pergolesi (1710–1736)

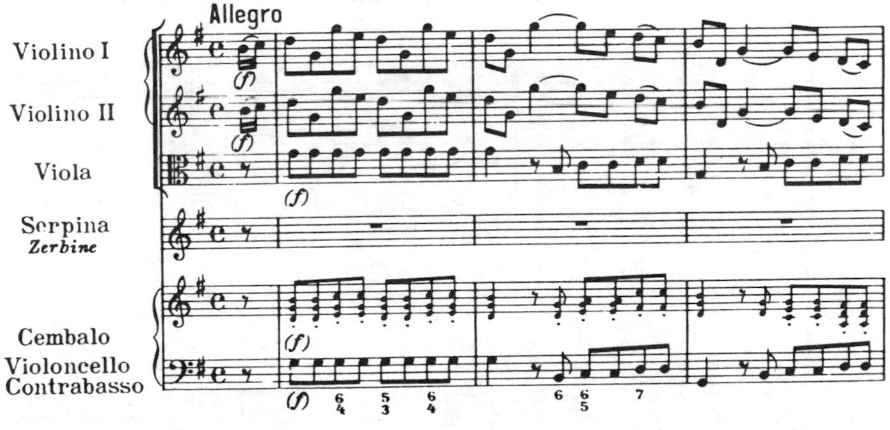
Allegro
Violino I
Violino II
Viola
Serpina
Zerbine
Cembalo
Violoncello
e Contrabasso

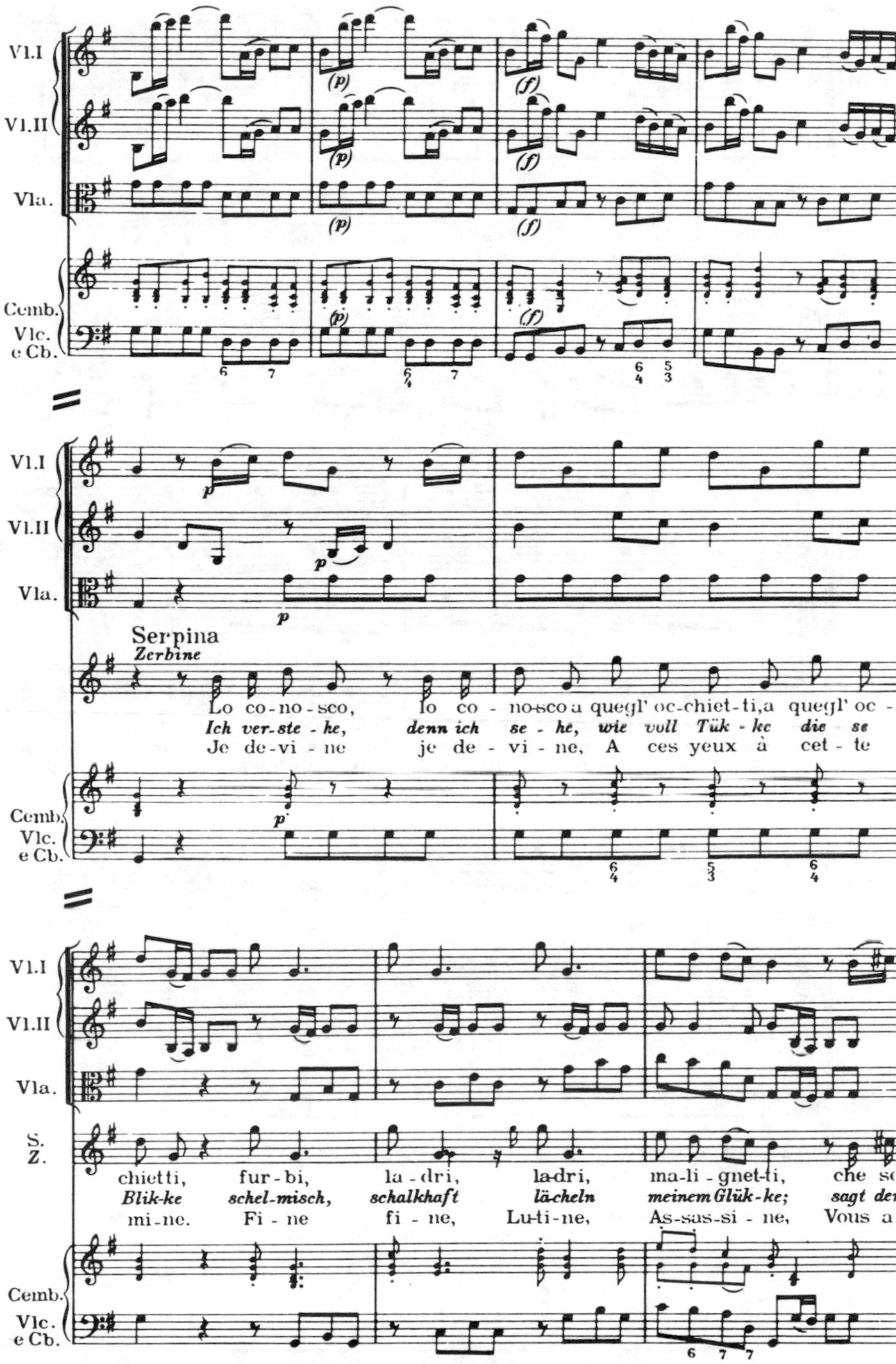
Vl.I
Vl.II
Vla.
Cemb.
Vlc. e Cb.
Serpina
Zerbine
Lo co-no-sco, lo co - no-sco a quegl' oc-chiet-ti, a quegl' oc -
Ich ver-ste - he, denn ich se - he, wie voll Tük - ke die - se
Je de-vi - ne je de - vi - ne, A ces yeux à cet - te
S.
Z.
chietti, fur-bi, la - dri, ladri, ma-li - gnet-ti, che se -
Blik-ke schel-misch, schalkhaft lächeln meinem Glük-ke; sagt der
mi-ne. Fi - ne fi - ne, Lu-ti-ne, As-sas-si - ne, Vous a -

33

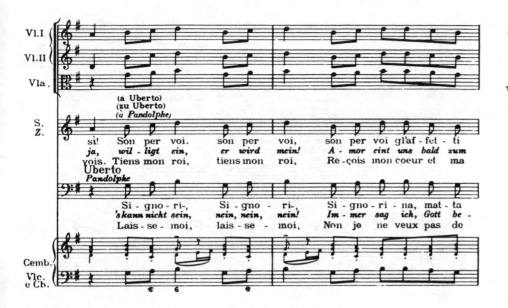

SERPINA:

Lo conosco, lo conosco a que gl'
    occhietti, a que gl' occhietti,
furbi, ladri, ladri, malignetti,
che seben voi dite no, no, no,
pur m'accennano di sì, sì, sì,
pur m'accennano di sì!

UBERTO:

Signorina, signorina, v'ingannate,
    v'ingannate!
Troppo, troppo, troppo, in alto voi
    volate!

SERPINA:

I know, I know from those little eyes,
    from those little eyes,
roguish, thieving, robbing, mischievous,
that although you say no, no, no,
you show me signs of yes, yes, yes,
you indicate to me, yes!

UBERTO:

Signorina, little lady, you are wrong, you
    are mistaken!
Too loud, too much, too loud, lower your
    voice!

Gl' occhi e Dio vi di con no, no, no.
ed un sogno è questo sì, sì, sì,
ed un sogno è questo sì!

SERPINA:
Ma perchè? Ma perchè?
Non sono io bella, graziosa, e spiritosa?
Su mirate leggiadria, leggiadria!
Vè che brio, che brio,
che maestà, che maestà!

UBERTO: (a parte)
Ah, costei mi va tentando,
quanto và che me la fa, che me la fa?

SERPINA: (a parte)
Ei mi par che va calando, va calando.

Risolvete!

UBERTO:
Eh, vanne via!

SERPINA:
Risolvete!

UBERTO:
Eh, matta sei!

SERPINA:
Son per voi gl' affetti miei,
e dovrete sposarme!
Dovrete, dovrete, dovrete, sposarme,
sposarme!

UBERTO:
Oh, ch' imbroglio, ch' imbroglio,
ch' imbroglio,
egl' è per me, egl' è per me!

SERPINA:
Lo conosco, sì, a que gl' occhietti,
furbi, ladri, malignetti!

My eyes and God tell you no, no, no,
and this yes, yes, yes, is a dream,
and this yes is a dream!

SERPINA:
But why? But for what reason?
Am I not lovely, graceful, and witty?
You admire prettiness, elegance!
See, what fire, what sprightliness,
what majesty, what majesty!

UBERTO: (aside)
Ah, this woman is trying [tempting] me,
how far is she going to trick me, to play
a trick on me?

SERPINA: (aside)
It seems to me that he is weakening, is
softening.
Resolve it!

UBERTO:
Oh, go away!

SERPINA:
Resolve it!

UBERTO:
Oh, you are insane!

SERPINA:
My love is for you,
and you should marry me!
You should, you ought to, you should,
marry me, marry me!

UBERTO:
Oh, what intrigue, what sharp practice,
what an entanglement,
this is for me, this is for me!

SERPINA:
I know, yes, from those little eyes,
roguish, thieving, mischievous!

UBERTO:
Signorina, signorina, v'ingannate!

SERPINA:
No, no, no, no, che se ben, che se ben,
che se ben voi dite no,
pur m'accennano di sì.

UBERTO:
V'ingannate!

SERPINA:
Ma perchè? Ma perchè?
Io son bella, graziosa, spiritosa!

UBERTO: (a parte)
Ah, costei mi va tentando!

SERPINA:
Va calando, sì, sì.
Vè che brio, che brio, che maestà, che
maestà!

UBERTO:
Quanto và, quanto và, quanto và che me
la fa?
La ralla, la ralla, la ralla, la ralala!
Eh, vanne via! Eh, matta sei!
Signorina, v'ingannate!
Signorina, no, no!
Oh, ch' imbrogl' egl' è per me!

SERPINA:
Via Signore, risolvete!
Son per voi gl' affetti miei, e dovrete sì,
sì.

UBERTO:
Quanto và, quanto và, quanto và che me
la fa!

SERPINA:
Io son bella, graziosa, spiritosa!

UBERTO:
La ralla, la ralla!

UBERTO:
Signorina, signorina, you are mistaken!

SERPINA:
No, no, no, no, indeed, indeed,
indeed, you say no,
still you indicate yes to me.

UBERTO:
You are mistaken!

SERPINA:
But why? For what reason?
I am beautiful, graceful, witty!

UBERTO: (aside)
Ah, this woman is indeed trying me!

SERPINA:
He is weakening, yes, yes.
See, what fire, what sprightliness, what
majesty, what majesty!

UBERTO:
How far is she going, to play a trick on
me?
La ra la, la ra la, etc.
Ah, go away! Oh, you are insane!
Signorina, you are mistaken!
Signorina, no, no!
Oh, what a muddle this is for me!

SERPINA:
Come, Lord, settle [the question]!
My love is for you, and it must be yes,
yes.

UBERTO:
How far is she going, to play a trick on
me?

SERPINA:
I am beautiful, graceful, witty!

UBERTO:
La ra la, la ra la!

SERPINA:
Vè che brio, vè che brio!

UBERTO:
Oh, ch' imbroglio! Oh, ch' imbroglio!

SERPINA: (a parte)
Va calando, sì, sì!

SERPINA: (à Uberto)
Son per voi, son per voi, son per voi gl'
  affetti miei,
e dovrete, sì, sì, sposarme, sposarme!

UBERTO:
Signori . . ., signori . . ., Signorina,
  matta sei!
Signorina, no, no, no, no!
Oh, ch' imbroglio, ch' imbroglio,
(repeated) egl' è per me, egl' è per
me!

Together

SERPINA:
Indeed, what fire, yes, what fire!

UBERTO:
Oh, what a muddle! Oh, what intrigue!

SERPINA: (aside)
He is weakening, yes, yes!

SERPINA: (to Uberto)
I am yours, I am yours, my love is
  yours, and
it must be yes, yes, marry me, marry
  me!

UBERTO:
Signori . . ., signori . . ., signorina,
  you are insane!
Signorina, no, no, no, no!
Oh, what an intrigue, what a muddle
  this is for me, this is for me!

Together

146. LE DEVIN DU VILLAGE Act I, Scene I
Jean Jacques Rousseau (1712-1778)

The stage setting has at one side the soothsayer's house, at the other side some trees and fountains, and at the back a hamlet.

Colette, crying and wiping her eyes with her apron.

Source: © 1924 by Ad. Henn, Geneva.

40

COLETTE: AIR.
J'ai perdu tout mon bonheur,
j'ai perdu mon serviteur.
Colin me délaisse,
Colin me délaisse.

J'ai perdu mon serviteur,
j'ai perdu tout mon bonheur.
Colin me délaisse,
Colin me délaisse.

hélas! il a pu changer!
je voudrais n'y plus songer.

COLETTE: AIR.
I have lost all my happiness,
I have lost my servant.
Colin forsakes me,
Colin forsakes me.

I have lost my servant,
I have lost all my happiness.
Colin forsakes me,
Colin forsakes me.

Alas! he could have changed!
I would rather not think about it any
        longer.

hélas! hélas!
hélas! hélas!
il a pu changer,
je voudrais n'y plus songer.

hélas! hélas!
j'y songe sans cesse,
j'y songe sans cesse.

J'ai perdu mon serviteur;
j'ai perdu tout mon bonheur.
Colin me délaisse,
Colin me délaisse.

J'ai perdu mon serviteur;
j'ai perdu tout mon bonheur.
Colin me délaisse,
Colin me délaisse.

RECITATIVE:

Il m'aimait autrefois et ce fut mon
malheur . . . mais quelle est donc
celle qu'il me préfère? elle est donc
bien charmante!
Imprudente bergère, ne crains tu point
les maux que j'éprouve en ce jour?

Colin a pu changer;
tu peux avoir ton tour . . .
que me sert d'y rêver sans cesse?

Rien ne peut guérir mon amour et tout
augmente ma tristesse.

AIR.
J'ai perdu mon serviteur;
j'ai perdu tout mon bonheur.
Colin me délaisse,
Colin me délaisse.

Alas! alas!
alas! alas!
He could have changed,
I would rather not think about it any
longer.

Alas! alas!
I think about it incessantly,
I dream about it incessantly.

I have lost my servant;
I have lost all my happiness.
Colin forsakes me,
Colin forsakes me.

I have lost my servant;
I have lost all my happiness.
Colin forsakes me,
Colin forsakes me.

RECITATIVE:

Once he loved me and this was my
misfortune . . . but who, then, is the
one whom he prefers to me? Indeed,
she is quite charming!
Imprudent shepherdess, do you not fear
at all the hurt that I am experiencing
today?
Colin could have changed;
you may have your turn . . .
of what use is it for me to dream about
it incessantly?
Nothing can cure my love and
everything increases my sadness.

AIR.
I have lost my servant;
I have lost all my happiness.
Colin forsakes me,
Colin forsakes me.

RECITATIVE.
Je veux le haïr; je le dois . . .
peut-être il m'aime encore . . .
pourquoi me fuir sans cesse?
Il me cherchait tant autrefois.
Le devin du canton fait ici sa demeure;
il sait tout; il saura le sort de mon
amour.
Je le vois et je veux m'éclaircir en ce
jour.

—J. J. Rousseau

RECITATIVE.
I want to hate him; I must do it . . .
perhaps he still loves me . . .
why do I flee incessantly?
He used to look for me so much.
The soothsayer of the canton lives here;
he knows everything; he will know the
fate of my love.
I see him, and I want [this] to be
clarified today.

147. CONCERTO FOR HARPSICHORD OR PIANO AND STRING ORCHESTRA, Op. 7, No. 5, in E♭ Major, mvt. 1
Johann Christian Bach (1735-1782)

Edited by Ákos Fodor

Source: European American Music Corporation, PA

46

148. CONCERTO NO. 27 FOR PIANO AND ORCHESTRA,
in B♭ Major, K. 595, mvt. 1
Wolfgang Amadeus Mozart (1756–1791)

54

59

Cadenza   [improvised], ending:

364

149. STRING QUARTET, Op. 5, No. 3, in A Major, mvt. 1
Franz Xaver Richter (1709-1789)

Breitkopf & Härtel, Wiesbaden

No recording of this quartet is available.

150. ORFEO ED EURIDICE, Act II, Scene 1
Christoph Willibald Gluck (1713-1787)

Ballo

Ballo

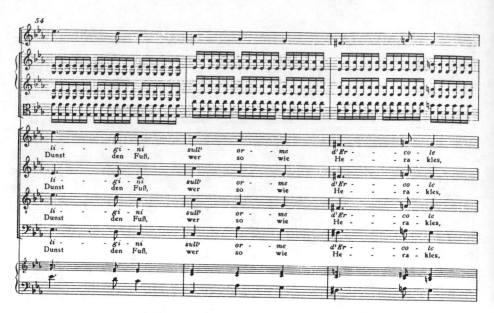

Coro

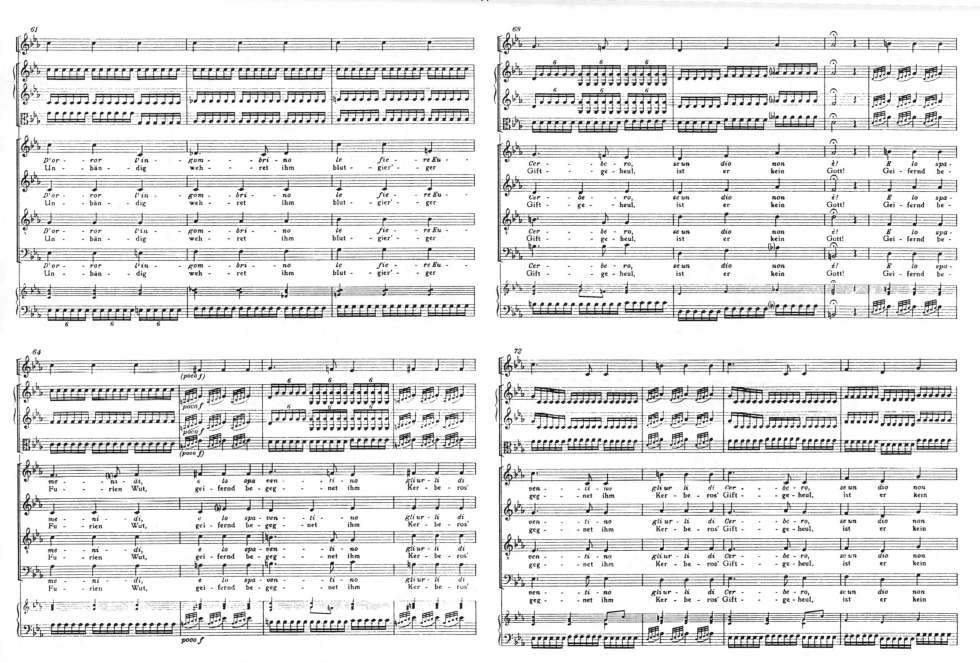

Segue il Ballo, girando intorno ad Orfeo per spaventarlo.
Es folgt ein Tanz, Orpheus umkreisend, um ihn zu schrecken.

Ballo

[turn quickly]

*) Kleingestochener Generalbaß dient als Stütze für Orchester II.

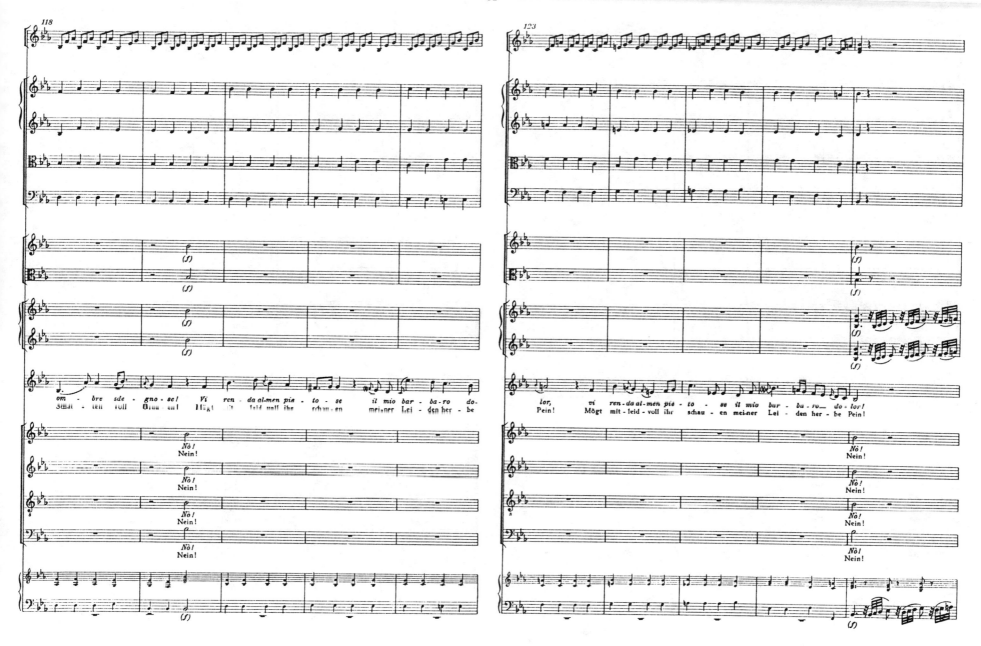

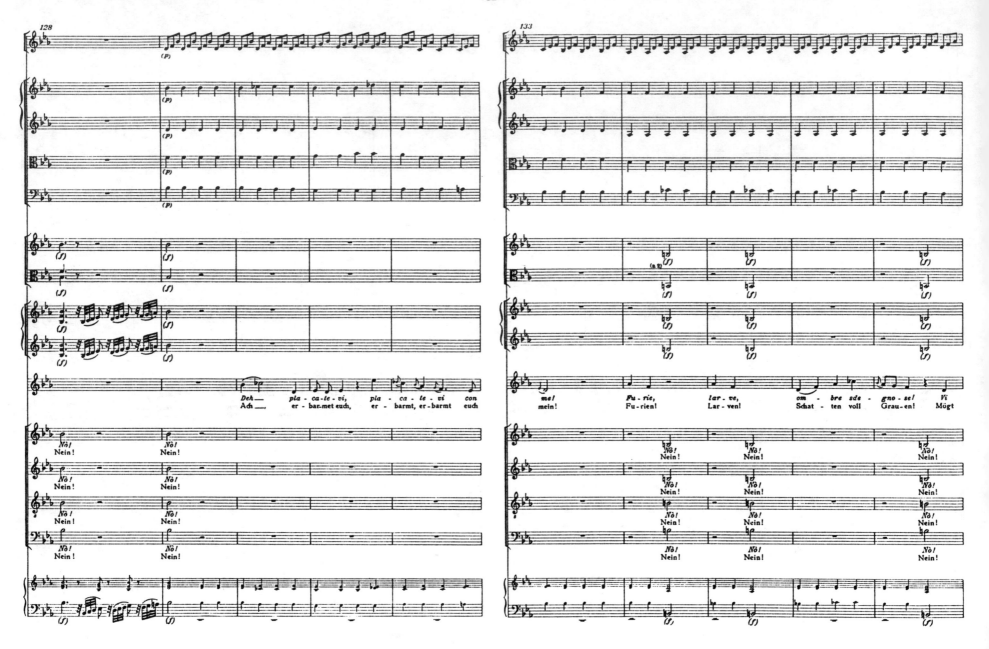

ren - da al - men pie - to - se   il mio bar - ba - ro do - lor!   Fu - rie,
mit - leid - voll ihr schau - en   mei - ner Lei - den her - be Pein!   Fu - rien!

tar - ve,   om - - bre sde - gno - se!   Vi   ren - da al - men pie - to - se   il mio
Lar - ven!   Schat - - ten voll Grau - en!   Mögt   mit - leid - voll ihr schau - en   mei - ner

Nò!   Nò!   Nò!
Nein!   Nein!   Nein!

Nò!   Nò!   Nò!
Nein!   Nein!   Nein!

Nò!   Nò!   Nò!
Nein!   Nein!   Nein!

Nò!   Nò!   Nò!
Nein!   Nein!   Nein!

BALLO (instrumental)

CHORUS:
Chi mai dell' Erebo fralle caligini sull'
orme d'Ercole e di Piritoo conduce il
piè?

BALLO (instrumental)

CHORUS:
Chi mai dell' Erebo fralle caligini sull'
orme d' Ercole e di Piritoo conduce il
piè?
D'orror l'ingombrino le fiere
Eumenidi, e lo spaventino gli urli di
Cerbero, se un dio non è!

E lo spaventino gli urli di Cerbero, se
un dio non è!

CHORUS REPEATS STANZA 2;
BALLO FOLLOWS

ORFEO:
Deh, placatevi con me.
Furie,   Larve,   Ombre sdegnose!
CHORUS INTERJECTS:
        No!   No!   No!

ORFEO continues:
Vi renda almen pietose
il mio barbaro dolor!
CHORUS: No! No! No!

BALLO (instrumental)

CHORUS:
Who would ever set forth from Erebus,
through the dark mists, in the
footsteps of Hercules and Pirithous?*

BALLO (instrumental)

CHORUS:
Who would ever set forth from Erebus,
through the dark mists, in the
footsteps of Hercules and Pirithous?
He would be obstructed by horror of
the bestial Eumenides, ** and he
would be frightened by the howling
of Cerberus, if he were not a god!
And he would be frightened by the
howling of Cerberus, if he were not a
god!

CHORUS REPEATS STANZA 2;
BALLO FOLLOWS

ORFEO:
Oh, please! Be gentle with me.
Furies,   Larvae,   disdainful shadows!
CHORUS:
        No!   No!   No!

ORFEO continues:
At least, may my cruel grief
make you merciful!
CHORUS: No! No! No!

*Pirithous, King of the Lapithae in
 Thessaly; friend of Theseus.
**Eumenides, euphemistic term
 meaning the Gracious Ones, which
 the Greeks used to refer to the Furies
 in order to propitiate them.

ORFEO:
Deh, placatevi con me.
Furie, Larve, Ombre sdegnose!
CHORUS:
No!   No!   No!
ORFEO:
Vi renda almen pietose il mio barbaro
    dolor!
    —Raniero de' Calzabigi

ORFEO:
Oh, please! Be gentle with me.
Furies,   Larvae,   scornful shadows!
CHORUS:
No!   No!   No!
ORFEO:
At least, let my barbarous grief make
    you merciful!

151. ORFEO ED EURIDICE, Act III, Scene 1, "Che farò senza Euridice?"
Christoph Willibald Gluck (1713-1787)

ben, do - vean - drò, che fa - rò, do - ve an - drò sen - za il mio ben?
sie, ach wo - hin, ach wo - hin, was be - ginn' ich oh - ne sie?

152. SONATA NO. 26, mvt. 2
Franz Joseph Haydn (1732-1809)

Menuetto al Rovescio.

Trio.

Menuetto da Capo.

Source: European American Music

Che farò senza Euridice?
Dove andrò senza il mio ben?
Euridice! Euridice!

Oh Dio! Rispondi!
Io son pure il tuo fedel.

Che farò senza Euridice?
Dove andrò senza il mio ben?
Euridice! Euridice!

Ah, non m'avanza più soccorso,
più speranza, nè dal mondo,
nè dal ciel!

Che farò senza Euridice?
Dove andrò senza il mio ben?
—Calzabigi

What will I do without Euridice?
Where will I go without my beloved?
Euridice! Euridice!

Oh, God! Answer!
I am still your faithful one.

What will I do without Euridice?
Where will I go without my beloved?
Euridice! Euridice!

Ah, no more help remains to me,
no more hope, neither from the world,
nor from heaven!

What will I do without Euridice?
Where will I go without my beloved?

153. STRING QUARTET, Op. 33, No. 2, mvt. 1
Franz Joseph Haydn (1732–1809)

154. SYMPHONY NO. 44 (Trauer), in E Minor, mvt. 3
Franz Joseph Haydn (1732–1809)

155. SYMPHONY NO. 104 (London), in D Major, mvt. 1
Franz Joseph Haydn (1732-1809)

Source: William J. Starr and George F. Devine, *Music Scores, Omnibus*, Part I, *Earliest Music Through the Works of Beethoven.* Copyright © 1964 Prentice-Hall, Inc., Englewood Cliffs, NJ.
Available recording: Nimbus NI-5096 (CD, original instruments)

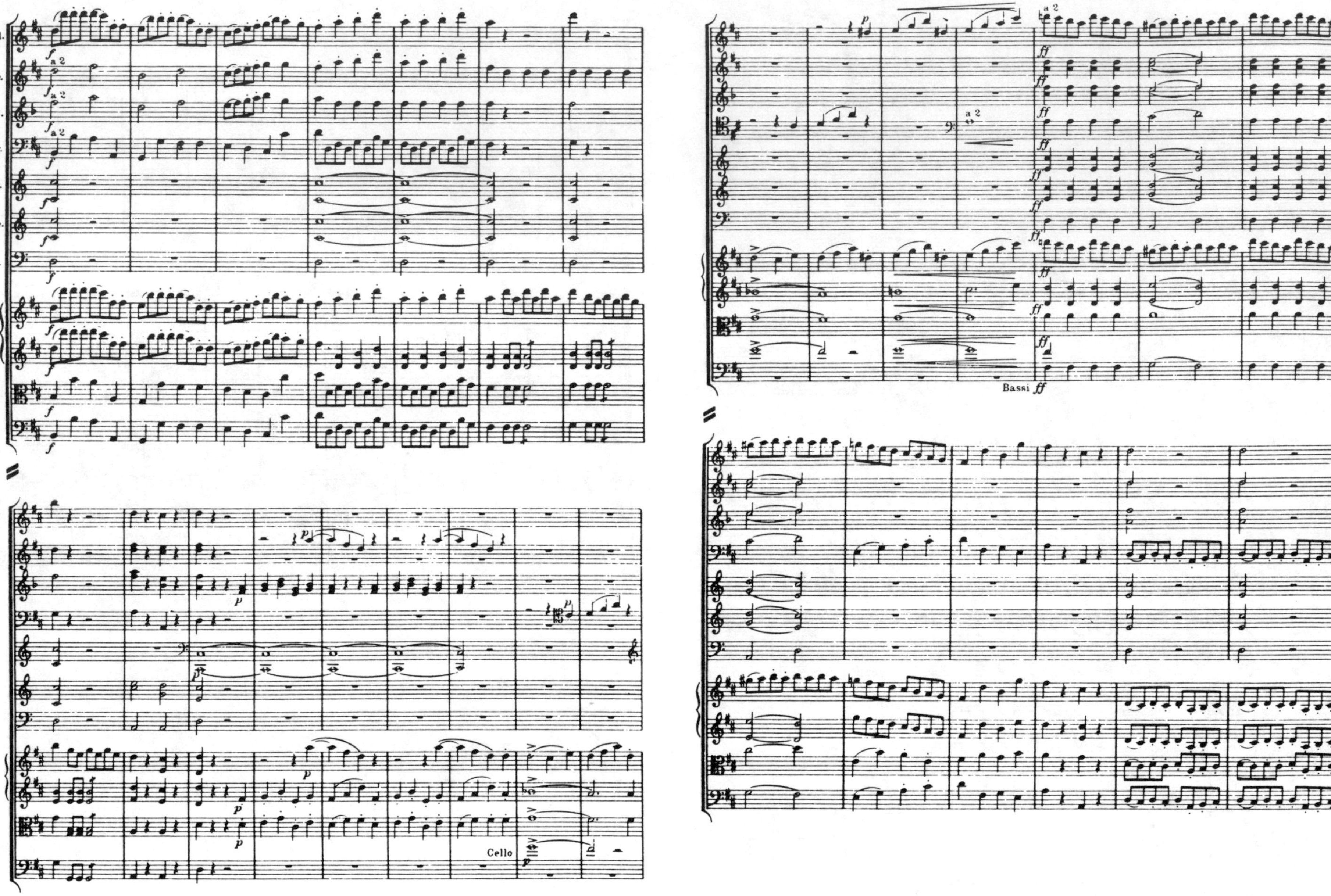
Fl.
Ob.
Cl.
Fg.
Cr.
Tbe.
Tp.
a 2
Cello
Bassi

156. LE NOZZE DI FIGARO, Act II, Terzetto: "Susanna, or via sortite!"
Wolfgang Amadeus Mozart (1756–1791)

"Le Nozze Di Figaro" (The Marriage of Figaro) Act II, Terzetto: "Susanna, or via sortite"
Libretto by Lorenzo Da Ponte. Music by W. A. Mozart. English Version—by Ruth and Thomas

l'o - ne - stà. Un' a - bi - to da spo - sa pro - van - do el - la si
that is why. A wed - ding dress was sent her, she has to try it
stà, pro - van - do el - la si stà
on, she has to try it on.
Count
p
Chia - ris - si - ma è la
I grasp the sit - u -
Susanna
p
Ca - pi - sco qual - che
A tick - lish sit - u -
Countess
p
Brut - tis - si - ma è la co - sa, brut - tis - si - ma è la
Your shame - ful ac - cu - sa - tion, your shame - ful ac - cu -
Count
co - sa, l'a - man - te qui sa - rà, chia - ris - si - ma è la
a - tion, her lov - er hides in - side, I grasp the sit - u -
f
co - sa, veg - gia - mo co - me va, ca - pi - sco
sa - tion, it can - not be de - nied, a tick - lish
f
co - sa, chi sa co - sa sa - rà, brut -
sa - tion se - vere - ly wounds my pride, your
f
co - sa, l'a - man - te qui sa - rà,
a - tion, her lov - er hides in - side.
f
p
p
qual - che co - sa, veg - gia - mo
sit - u - a - tion, he took us
p
tis - si - ma è la co - sa, chi sa co -
im - pu - dent ac - cu - sa - tion is base - less
p
chia - ris - si - ma è la co - sa, l'a - man - te
Dis - grace - ful sit - u - a - tion! I took them
f
p
f
p

157. IL DON GIOVANNI, Excerpts
Wolfgang Amadeus Mozart (1756-1791)
a. Overture

Anderer (Konzert-) Schluß der Ouvertura:

*) Anderer (Konzert-) Schluß der Ouvertura siehe S. 27; vgl. auch Vorwort.

Alternate (Concert) ending of Overture.

segue Introduzione (N° 1, S. 28)

b. Act I, No. 4, Aria: "Madamina"

157b. Don Giovanni Opera in Two Acts: "Madamina, il Catalogo è questo," music by W. A. Mozart, G. Schirmer, Inc., New York, NY.

126

Madamina! Il catalogo è questo,
delle belle, che amò il padron mio!

Un catalogo egli è ch'ho fatto io:
Osservata, leggete con me!

In Italia sei cento e quaranta,
in Alemagna due cento trent'una;
cento in Francia, in Turchia novant'una,

ma, ma in Ispagna, son già mille e tre!

V'han fra queste contadine, cameriere, citadine,
v'han contesse, baronesse, marchesane, principesse,
e v'han donne d'ogni grado,

d'ogni forma, d'ogni età.

Nella bionda egli ha l'usanza
di lodarla gentilezza . . .
nella bruna la costanza,
nella bianca la dolcezza.

Vuol d'inverno la grassotta,
vuol d'estate la magrotta,
e la grande maestosa,
e la grande maestosa.

La piccina, la piccina, . . .
[these 2 words are repeated 6 more times]
è ognor vezzosa;
[these 3 words are repeated twice more]

Delle vecchie fa conquista
per piacer di porle in lista;

sua passion predominante
è la giovin principante;

Little lady! This is the catalog
of the beautiful [women] that my master loved.
It is a catalog that I have made:
Observe, read with me!

In Italy, six hundred and forty,
in Germany, two hundred thirty-one;
a hundred in France, in Turkey ninety-one,
but in Spain, there are already a thousand and three!

Among these there are peasants, maids, townswomen,
there are countesses, baronesses, marchionesses, princesses,
and there are ladies of every [social] class,
of every figure, of every age.

With blonds he has the habit
of praising gentility . . .
with brunettes, loyalty,
with white-haired ladies, sweetness.

In winter he desires the fat one,
in summer he wants the lean one,
and the tall, majestic one,
and the tall, majestic one.

The little one, the tiny one, . . .

is always graceful;

He makes conquest of the old ones
for the pleasure of putting them on the list;
his prevailing passion
is the young beginner;

Non si picca, se sia ricca,

se sia bruta, se sia bella,

se sia ricca, bruta,
se sia bella,
purchè porti la gonnella.
Voi sapete quel che fa.
—Da Ponte

It doesn't matter to him, whether she is rich,
whether she is ugly, whether she is beautiful,
whether she is rich, ugly,
whether she is beautiful,
provided she wears the skirt.
You know what he does.

158. SYMPHONY NO. 40, in G Minor, K. 550, mvt. 1
Wolfgang Amadeus Mozart (1756-1791)

The Oboe and Clarinet parts printed in the two systems at the top were added later by Mozart to replace the Oboe part in the fourth system.

Source: Dover Publications, Inc., Mineola, N.Y.

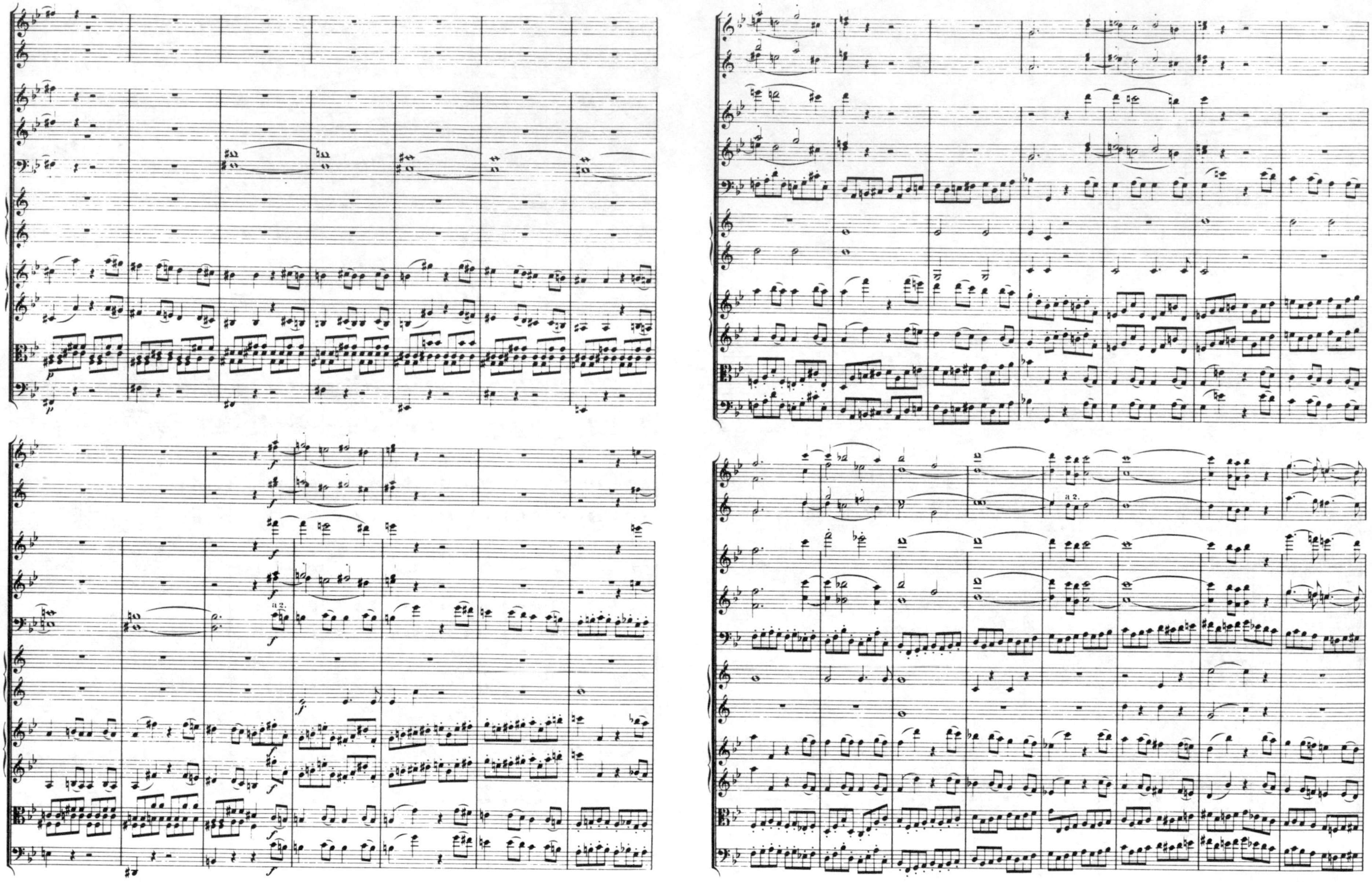
a 2.
a 2.

137

159. SONATA in C Minor, K. 457
Wolfgang Amadeus Mozart (1756–1791)

Allegro (after the Autograph)
Molto Allegro (after Artaria and Götz)

Source: Theodore Presser Company, Bryn Mawr, PA

Only the first movement is on the record set.

* 1st ed.: 🎵 . ** 1st ed.: 🎵

("All the performance indications according to the oldest edition; the Autograph contains them mostly only in the variations of the theme." – B. & H. "Urtext" ed.)

* 1st ed. :

* 1st ed.:

Molto allegro (after the Autograph)
Allegro assai (after Artaria and Götz)

* Artaria and Götz:

160. DAS GRAB, Lied
Johann R. Zumsteeg (1760-1802)

Langsam.

Das Grab ist tief und stil-le, und schau-der-haft sein Rand. Es deckt mit schwarzer Hül-le ein un-be-kann-tes Land.

Gregg International White Swan House, Godstone, Surrey, England

Das Grab ist tief und stille,	The grave is deep and still,
und schauderhaft sein Rand.	and its brink is dreadful.
Es deckt mit schwarzer Hülle	It is an unknown land covered
ein bekanntes Land.	with black wrapping.
Das Lied der Nachtigallen	The song of the nightingale
Tönt nicht in seinen Schooss.	does not sound in its branches.
Der Freundschaft Rosen fallen	The friendship of roses falls
Nur auf des Hügels Moos.	only on the moss of the hills.
Verlassne Bräute ringen	The forsaken bride wrings
Umsonst die Hände wund.	her sore hands in vain.
Der Waise klagen dringen	The complaint of the orphan does not
Nicht in der Tiefe Grund.	penetrate to the depth of the ground.
Doch sonst au keinem Orte	Yet in no other place
Wohnt die ersehnte Ruh';	does the longed-for rest abide;
Nur durch die dunkle Pforte	only through the dark portal
Geht man der Heimat zu.	does one go [to his] home.
Das arme Herz, hienieden	The poor heart, on this earth
Von manchem Sturm bewegt,	moved by many a storm,
Erlangt den wahren Frieden	attains lasting peace
Nur, wo es nicht mehr schlägt.	only when it beats no more.
—Johann Gaudenz von Salis	

* Artaria and Götz:

161. TAUNTON, Fuging Tune
William Billings (1746–1800)

The American Musicological Society and The Colonial Society of Massachusetts

2. For Thee, my God, the living God,
My thirsty Soul doth pine:
O! when shall I behold thy Face,
Thou Majesty Divine?

3. Tears are my constant Food, while thus
Insulting Foes upbraid:
"Deluded Wretch! where's now thy God?
And where his promis'd Aid?"

4. I sigh whene'er my musing Thoughts
Those happy Days present,
When I with Troops of pious Friends
Thy Temple did frequent:

5. When I advanc'd with Songs of Praise,
My solemn Vows to pay;
And led the joyful sacred Throng,
That kept the festal Day.

6. Why restless, why cast down, my Soul?
Trust God; and He'll employ
His Aid for thee, and change these Sighs
To thankful Hymns of Joy.

7. My Soul's cast down, O God; but thinks
On Thee and Sion, still;
From Jordan's Bank, from Hermon's Heights,
And Missar's humbler Hill.

8. One Trouble calls another on;
And, bursting o'er my Head,
Fall spouting down, till round my Soul,
A roaring Sea is spread.

9. But when thy Presence, Lord of Life,
Has once dispell'd this Storm,
To Thee I'll midnight Anthems sing,
And all my Vows perform.

10. God of my Strength, how long shall I,
Like one forgotten mourn,
Forlorn, forsaken, and expos'd
To my Oppressors Scorn?

11. My Heart is pierc'd, as with a Sword,
Whil'st thus my Foes upbraid;
"Vain Boaster, where is now thy God?
And where his promis'd Aid?"

12. Why restless, why cast down, my Soul?
Hope still; and thou shalt sing
The Praise of Him who is thy God,
Thy Health's eternal Spring.

162. WHEN JESUS WEPT, Canon
William Billings (1746–1800)

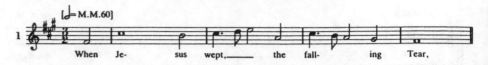

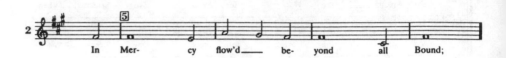

Source: The American Musicological Society and the Colonial Society of Massachusetts.

163. "MY GEN'ROUS HEART DISDAINS," Rondo
Francis Hopkinson (1737–1791)

From Da Capo Press, New York, N.Y.

151

or an eye; For a braid - ed lock of

hair, Curse my for - tune, curse my for - tune and de - spair,

Curse my for - tune and de - spair; My still un - cer - tain is to

- mor - row, Not quite cer - tain is to - day, Shall I

waste my time in sor - row; Shall I lan - guish life a - way;

All be - cause a cru - el maid Hath not love with love re - paid,

Hath not love with love re - paid................................... My

164. TRIO IN E♭ MAJOR, Op. 3, No. 1
for two violins and violoncello
John Antes (1740–1811)

ed. and arr. by Thor Johnson,
Donald M. McCorkle

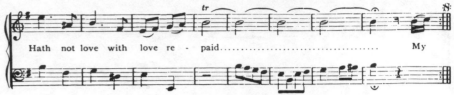

Adagio

THREE TRIOS. © Copyright 1961 by Boosey & Hawkes, Inc. Copyright renewed, 1989. Used by permission.

Only the first movement is on the record set.

154

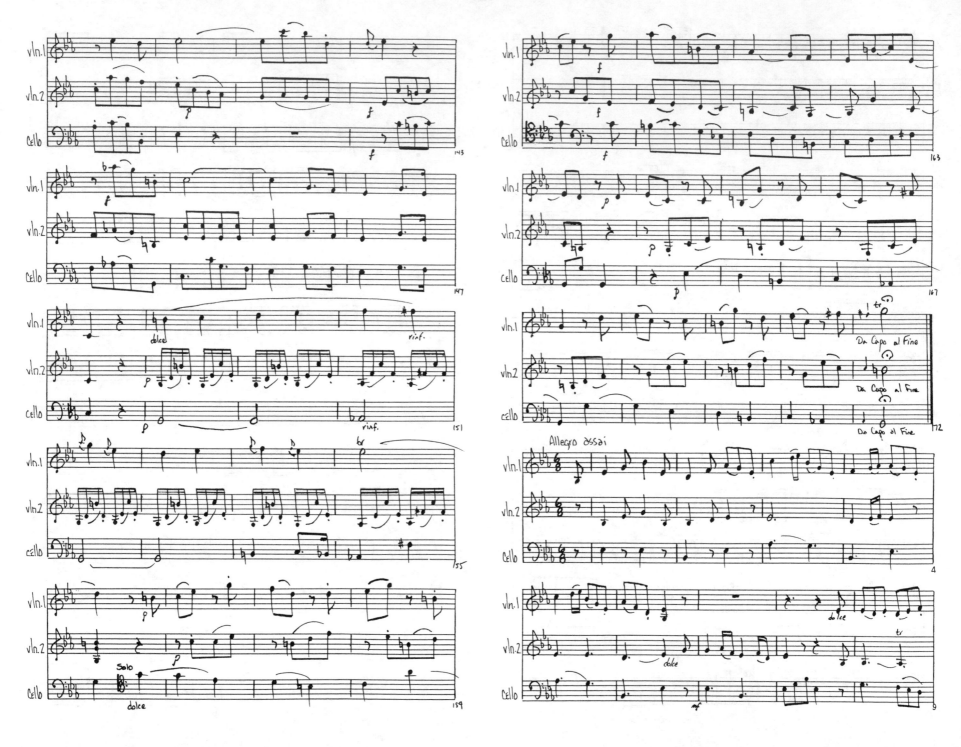

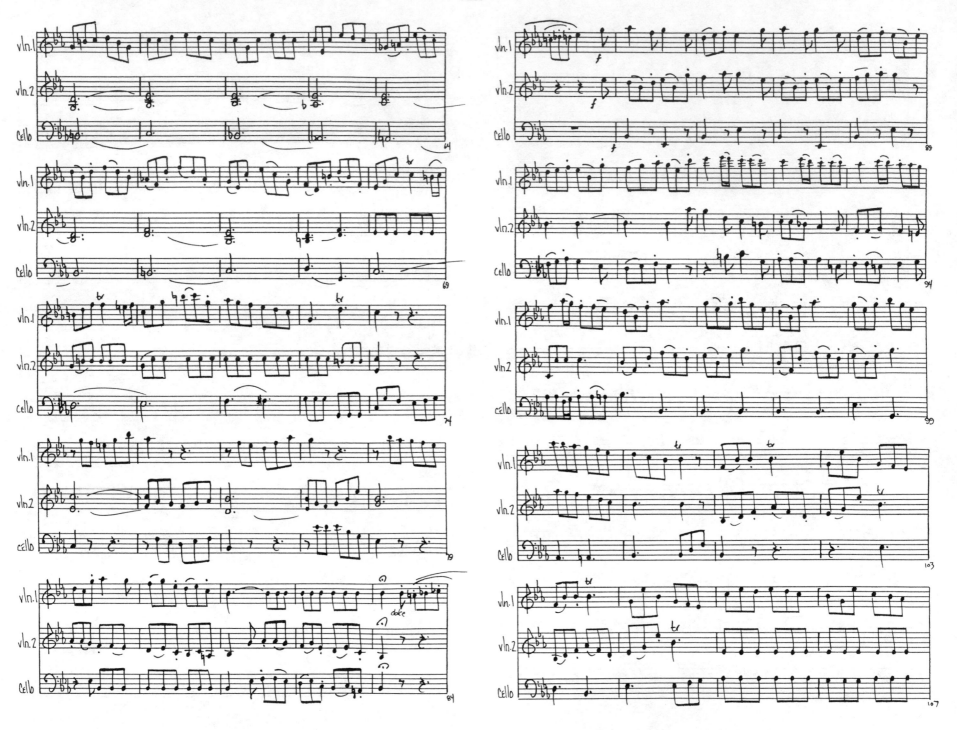

165. ARIA AND ANTHEM
John Antes (1740–1811)

a. "Go, Congregation, Go"

Christian Gregor
(1723–1801)

Edited and arranged by
Donald M. McCorkle

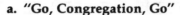

Note: *tr* indicates the points at which double trills (in the top voices simultaneously) are used in the original accompaniment. Since it is impossible to transcribe this device for keyboard, it may be more satisfactory to omit all such trills.

see, ____ go and see thy Sav - iour, thy Sav ____ iour

in ____ Geth - se - ma - ne: There is a

scene, a scene which with a maze ____ must ____ strike ____ thee;

There, as - ton - ished gaze, thy Mak - er
(Mas - ter)

prays. thy Mak - er prays. ____
(Mas - ter)

b. "Surely He Has Borne Our Griefs"

Isaiah 53: 4, 5

Edited and arranged by
Donald M. McCorkle

Grave
(sempre *p*)

Soprano — Sure - ly He has borne our
(hath)

Alto — Sure - ly He has borne our
(hath)

Tenor — Sure - ly He has borne our
(hath)

Bass — Sure - ly He has borne our
(hath)

Grave
(sempre *p*)

163

griefs and car - - - ried our sor - rows.

griefs and car - - - ried our sor - rows.

griefs and car - - - ried our sor - rows.

griefs and car - - - ried our sor - rows.

gress - - - ions, He was bruis - ed for

gress - - - ions, He was bruis - ed for

gress - - - ions, He was bruis - ed for

gress - - - ions, He was bruis - ed for

A

He was wound - ed for our trans -

He was wound - ed for our trans -

He was wound - ed for our trans -

He was wound - ed for our trans -

our in - i - qui - ties;

our in - i - qui - ties;

our in - i - qui - ties;

our in - i - qui - ties;

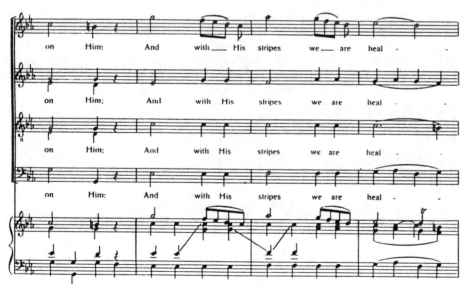

166. SONATA in C Minor, Op. 35, No. 3, mvt. 1
Jan Ladislav Dussek (1760–1812)

Bearbeitet von Hans Albrecht

Source: Kistner & Siegel & Company, West Germany

167

167. NOCTURNE NO. 5, in B♭ Major
John Field (1782–1837)

Nocturne No. 5 in B-Flat Major—by John Field. Reprinted by Permission of G. Schirmer, Inc.

168. ECLOGUE XXXVI, Op. 66, No. 6
Václav Jan Tomášek (1774–1850)

Source: European American Music Distributors, PA

*) Orig. ♩.

*) Orig.   **) Orig.

*) Orig. *f*, anche bat. 66, bat. 68, 69.

Da Capo fin che al Fine

169. IMPROMPTU, Op. 7, No. 3
Jan Václav Voříšek (1791–1825)

170. PIANO SONATA NO. 23, in F Minor, Op. 57, "Appassionata," mvt. 1
Ludwig van Beethoven (1770-1827)

Allegro assai

*) In second part of 1ˢᵗ theme and the following passages based thereon, the slurs in autogr. and orig. edition are by no means uniform; this divergence has been rectified throughout.

Source: Music Sales Corporation, New York, N.Y.

*) In autogr. and orig.ed., the slurs in the 2. theme
   and its repetitions are also very dissimilar; here too
   this disagreement has been corrected throughout.

*) In autograph and orig.edition e^2 instead of fb^2.
**) And also octave e–e^1 (above on the contrary fb^3).

*) In the autograph and the original edition,
inner voice Bb (not G).

*) In the autograph and the original edition
the prefix to the trill is lacking; cf. bar 44.

*) f only in autograph, not in orig. edition.

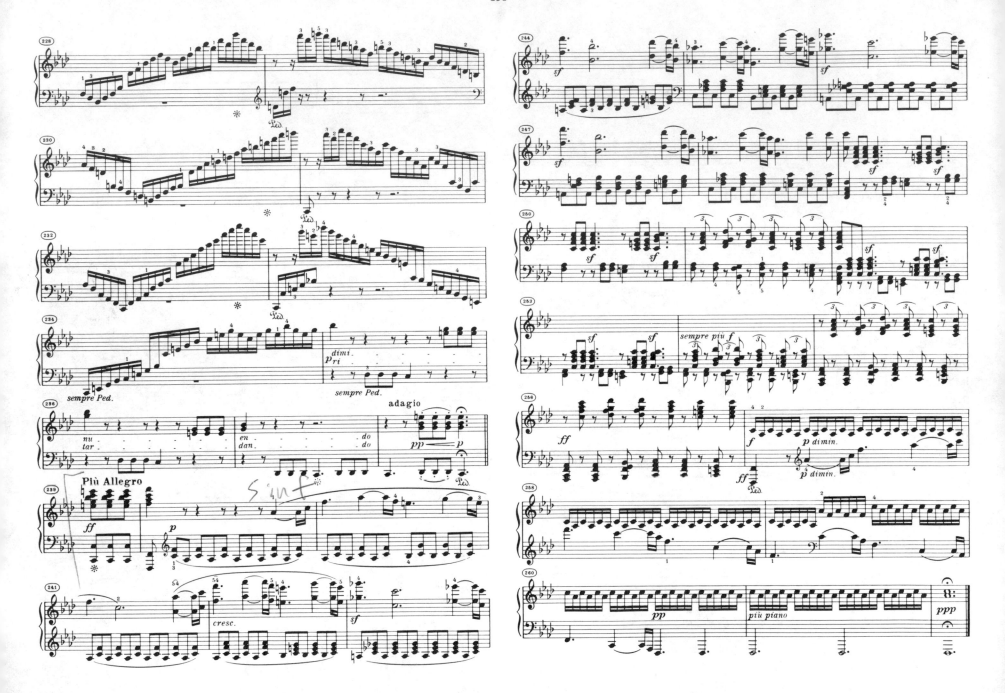

171. SYMPHONY NO. 3 (Eroica), in E♭ Major, mvts. 1, 4
Ludwig van Beethoven (1770–1827)

Permission by Edwin F. Kalmus & Co., Inc., Boca Raton, FL

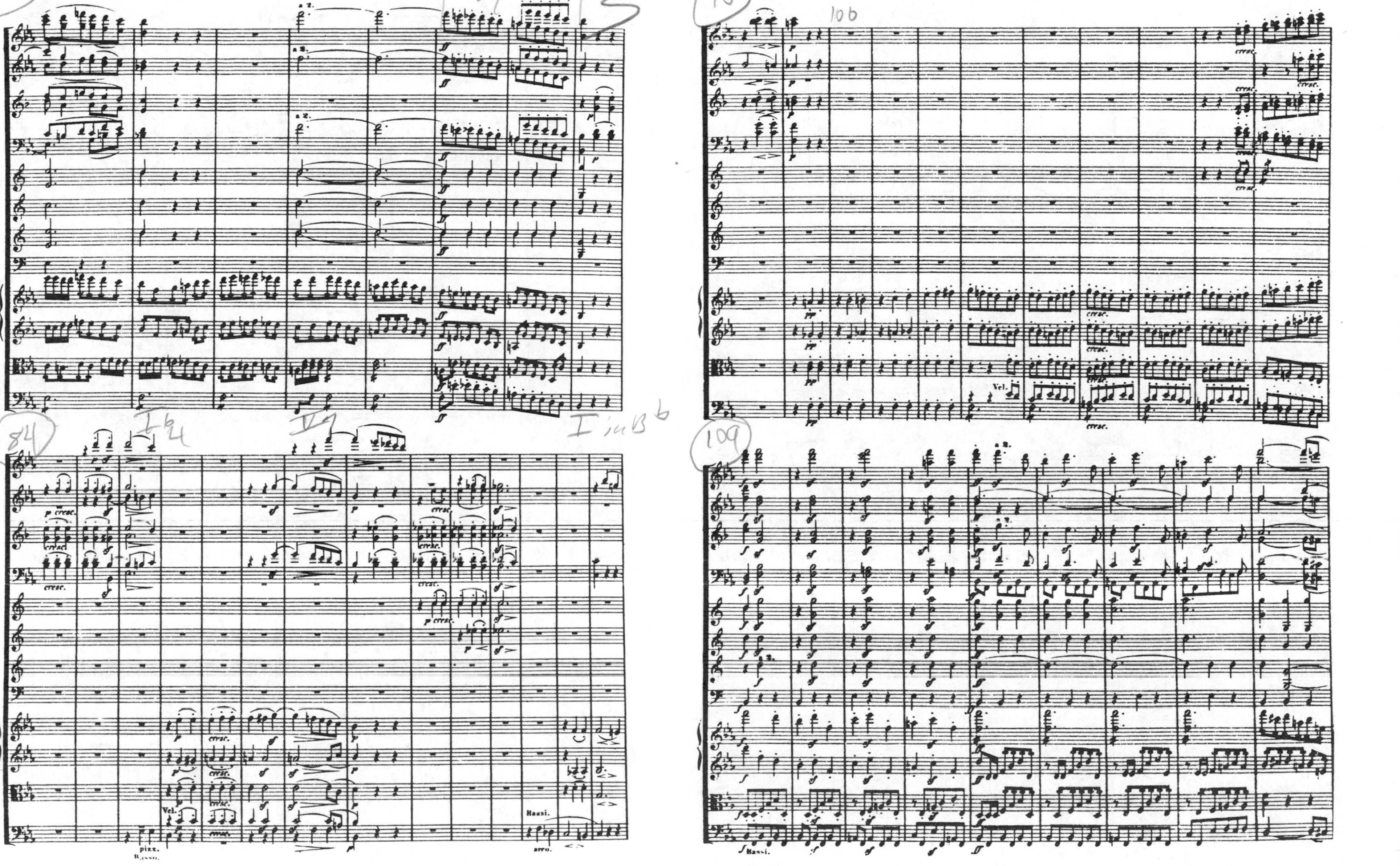
a 2.
cresc.
Vel.
pizz.
Bassi
arco

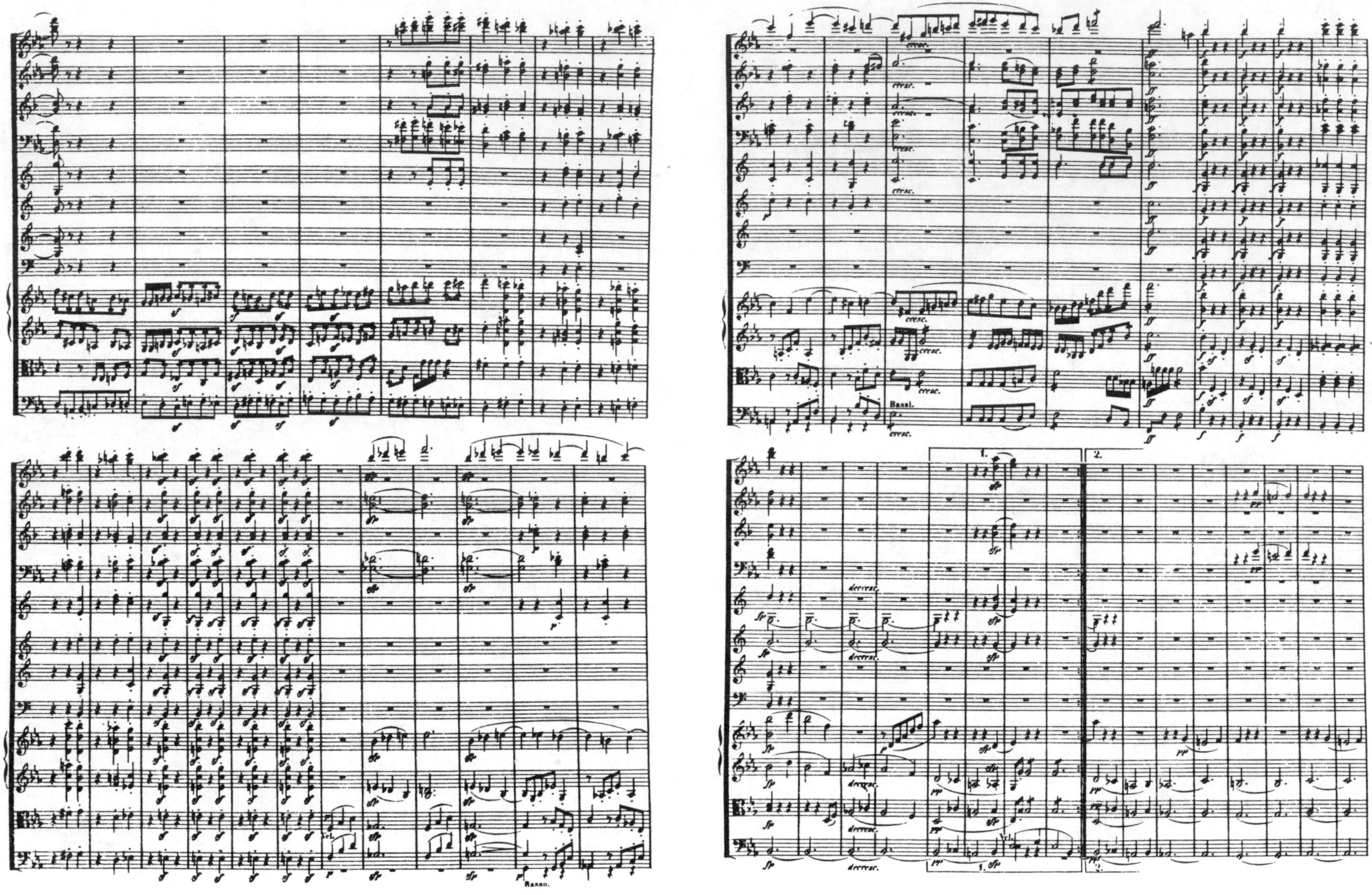
cresc.
Bassi.
decresc.
Basso.
1.
2.

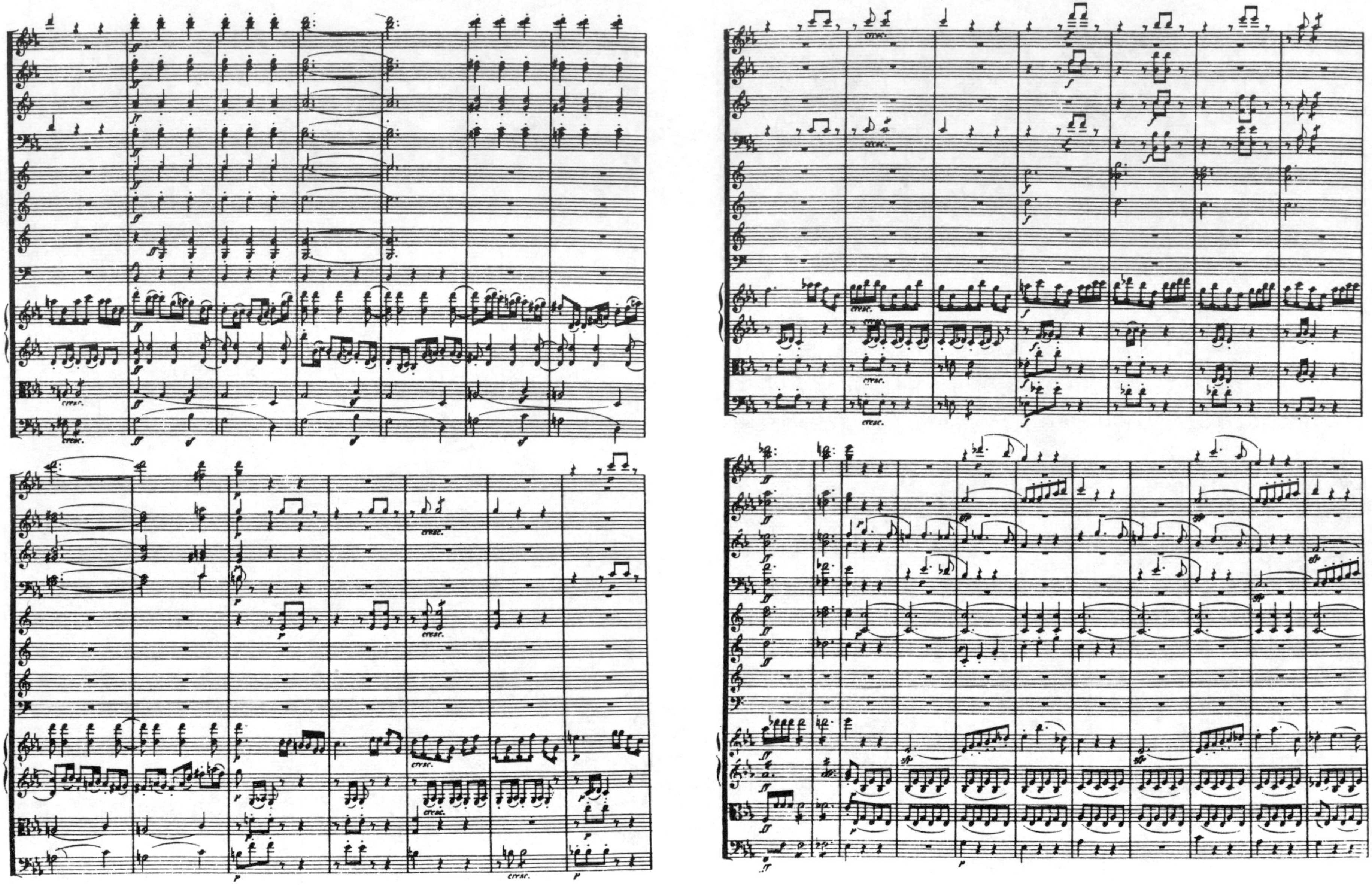
cresc.

232

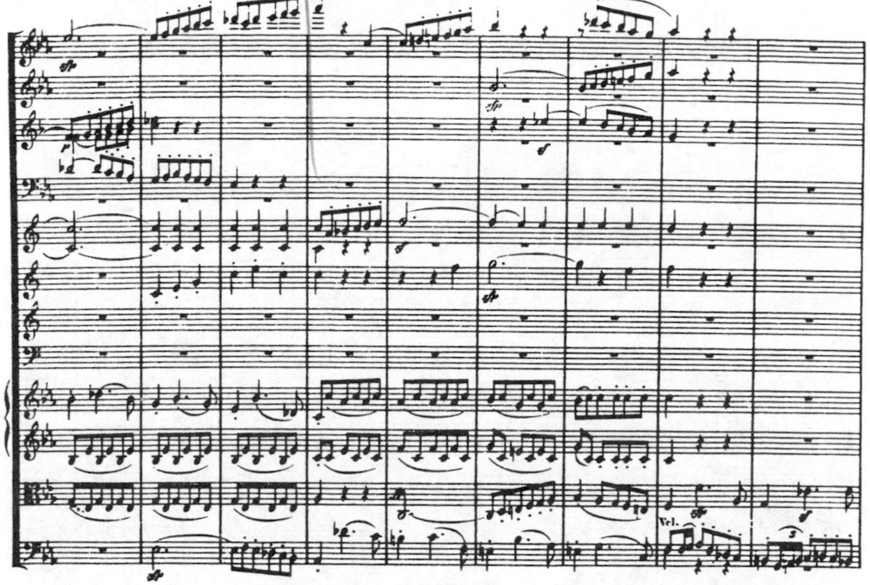

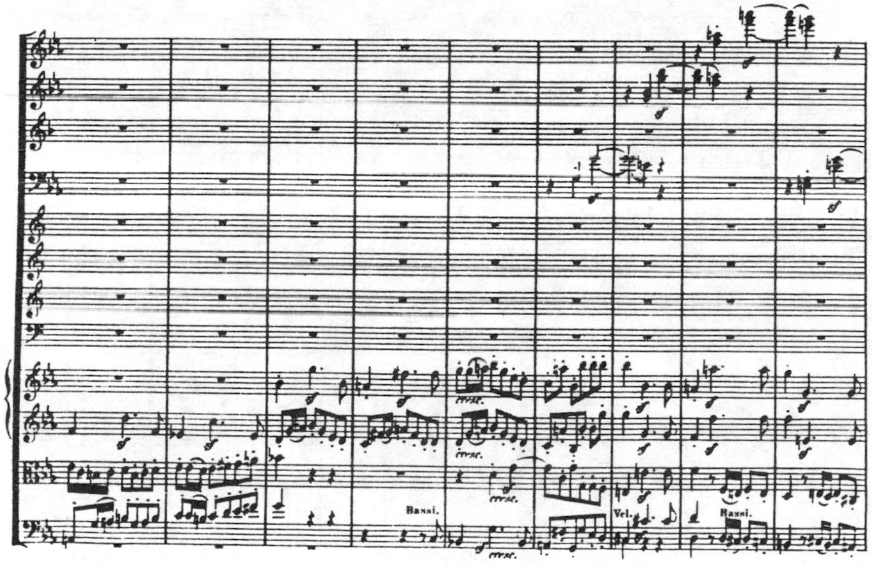

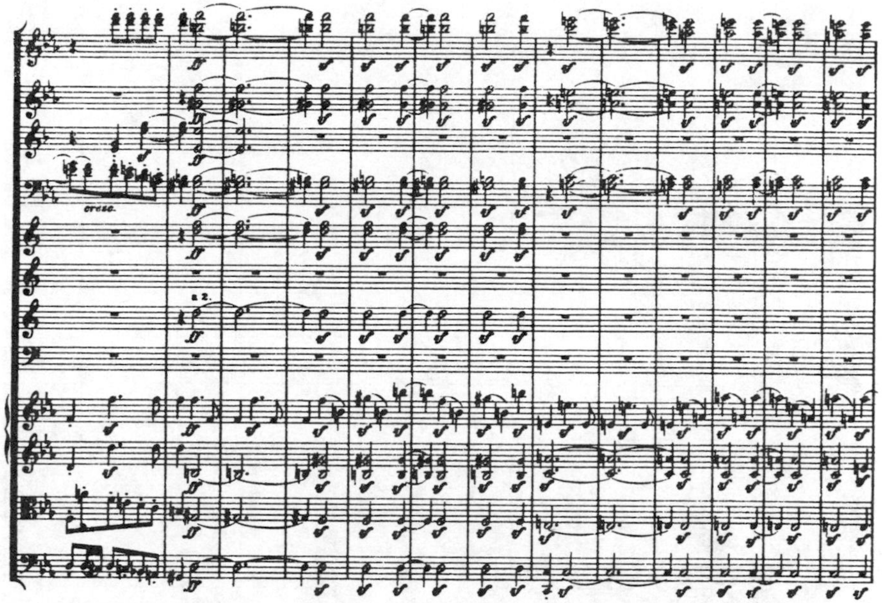

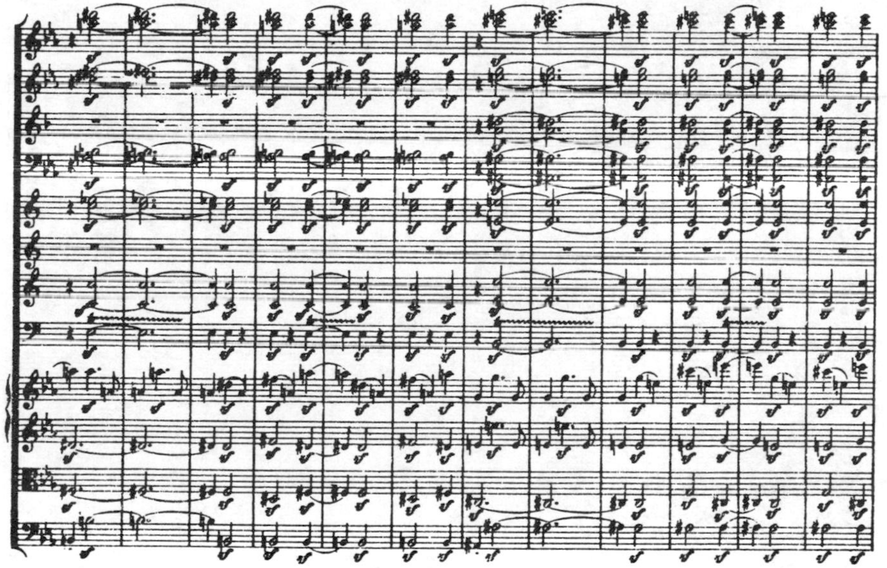

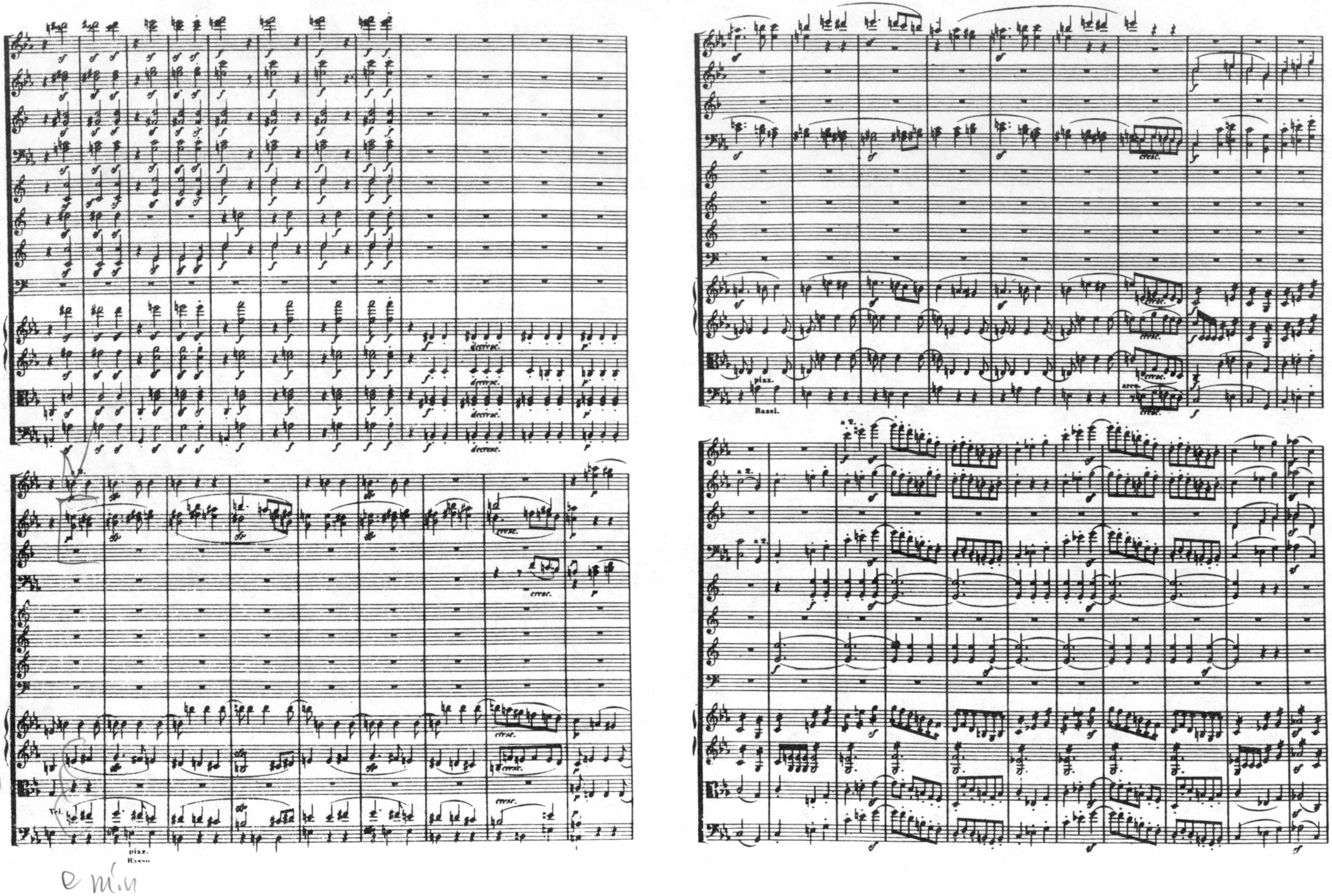
decresc.
cresc.
pizz.
Bassi
arco
a 2.
pizz.
Basso

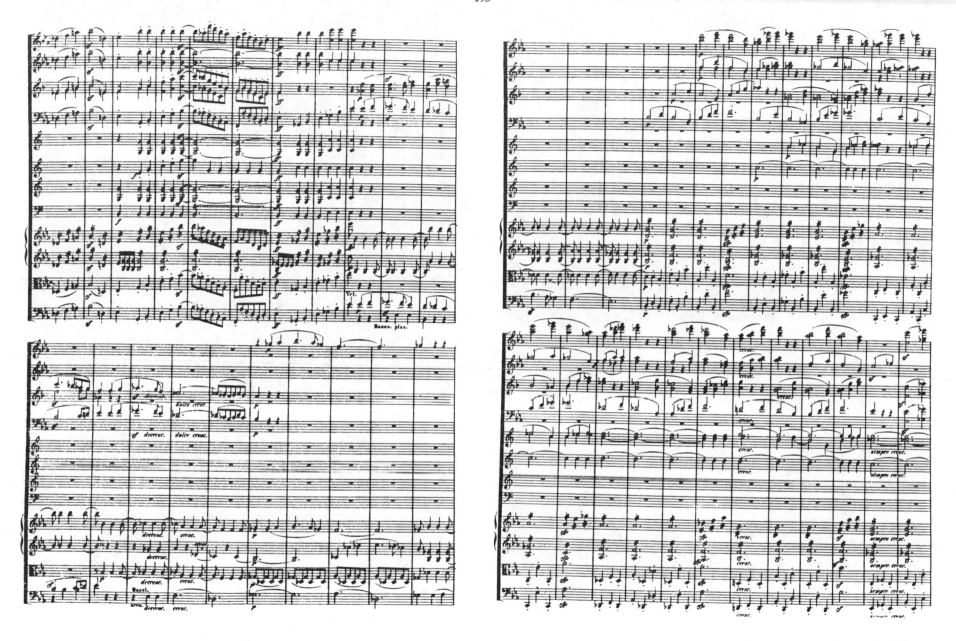

"Horn too early"

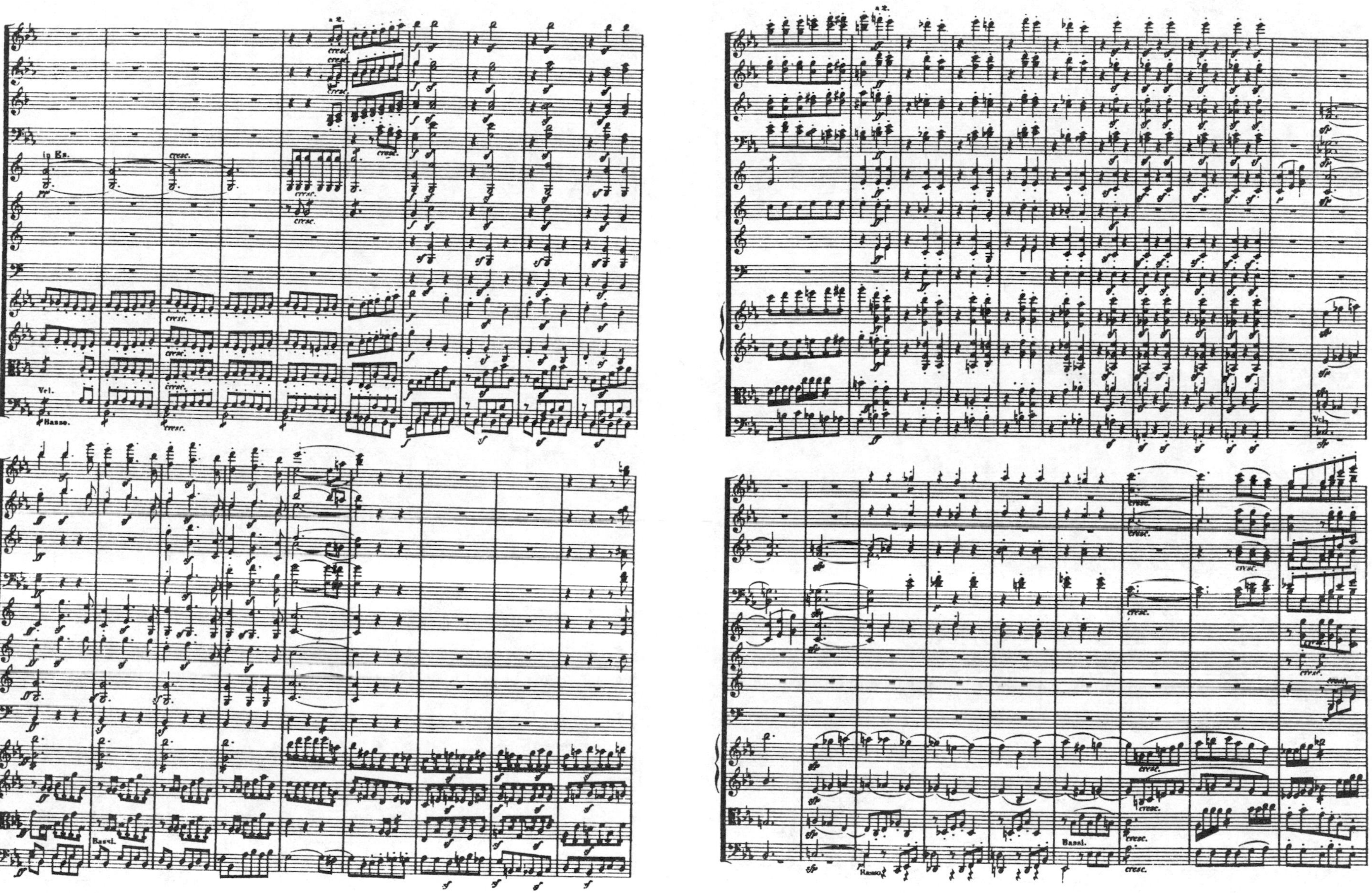
a 2.
in Es.
cresc.
Vcl.
Basso
Bassi

Coda

199

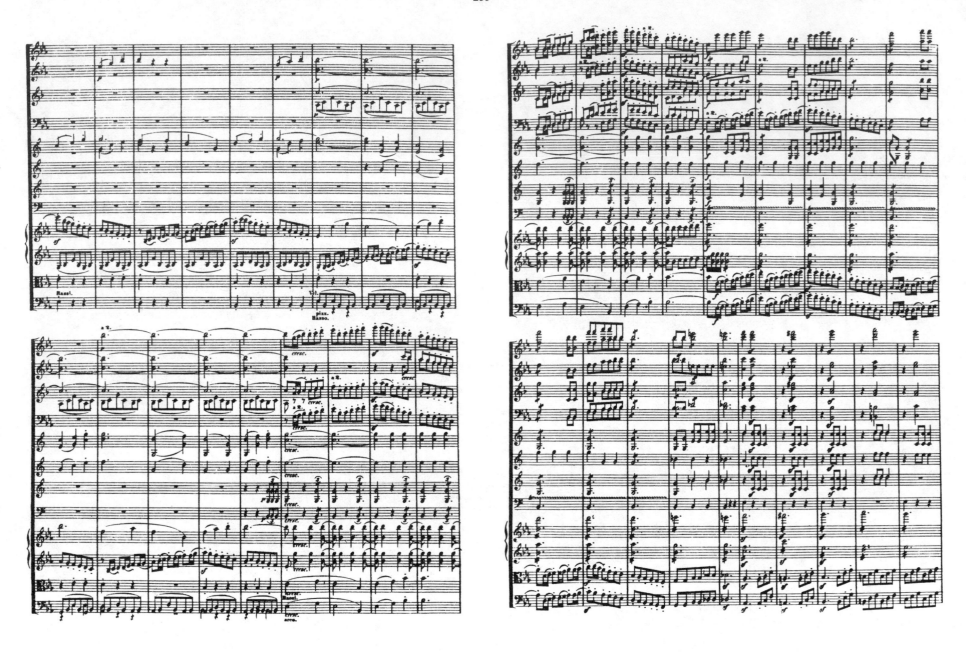

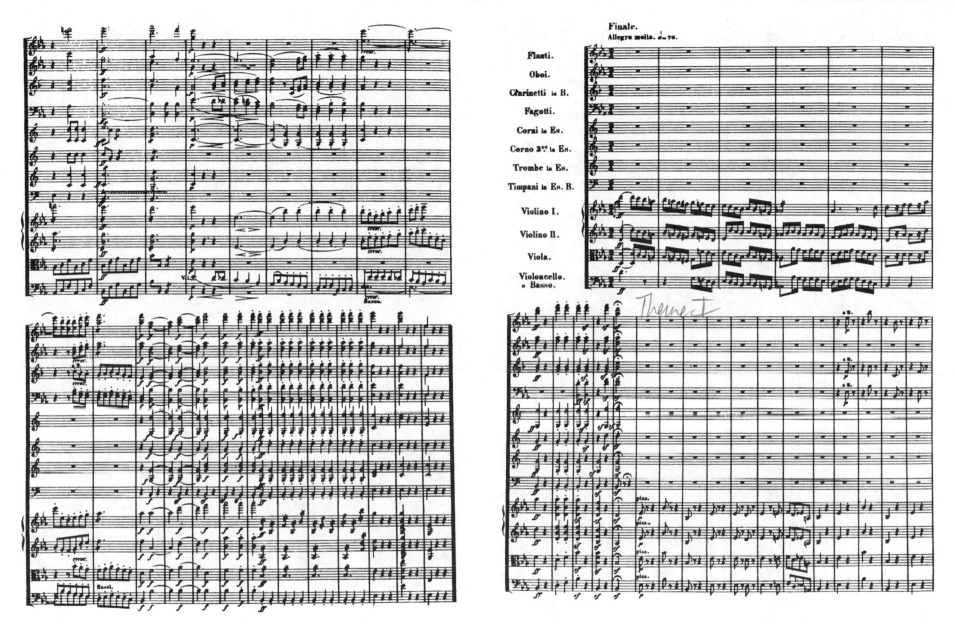

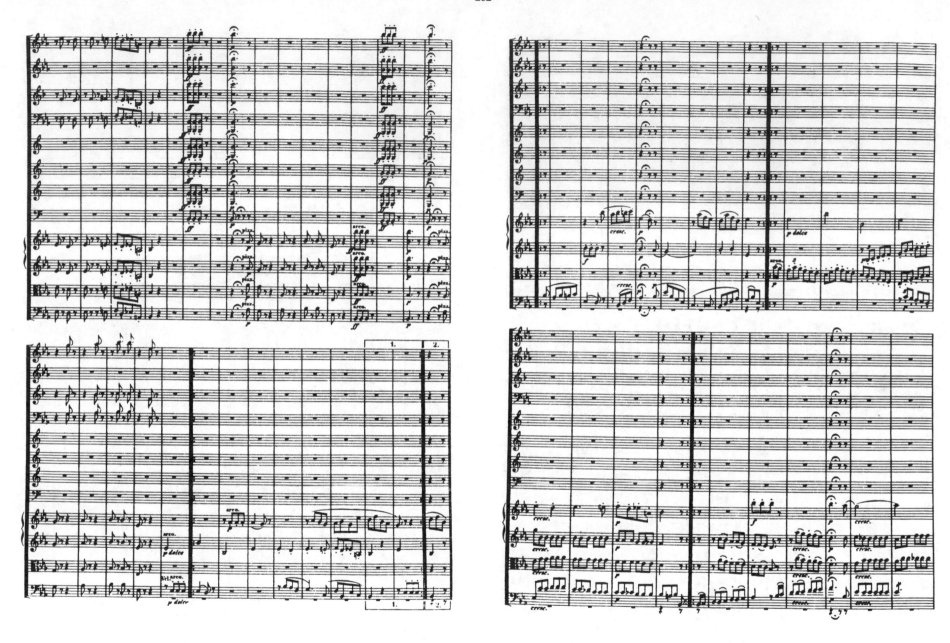

Thy. II

Var. 3 (Contradance theme)

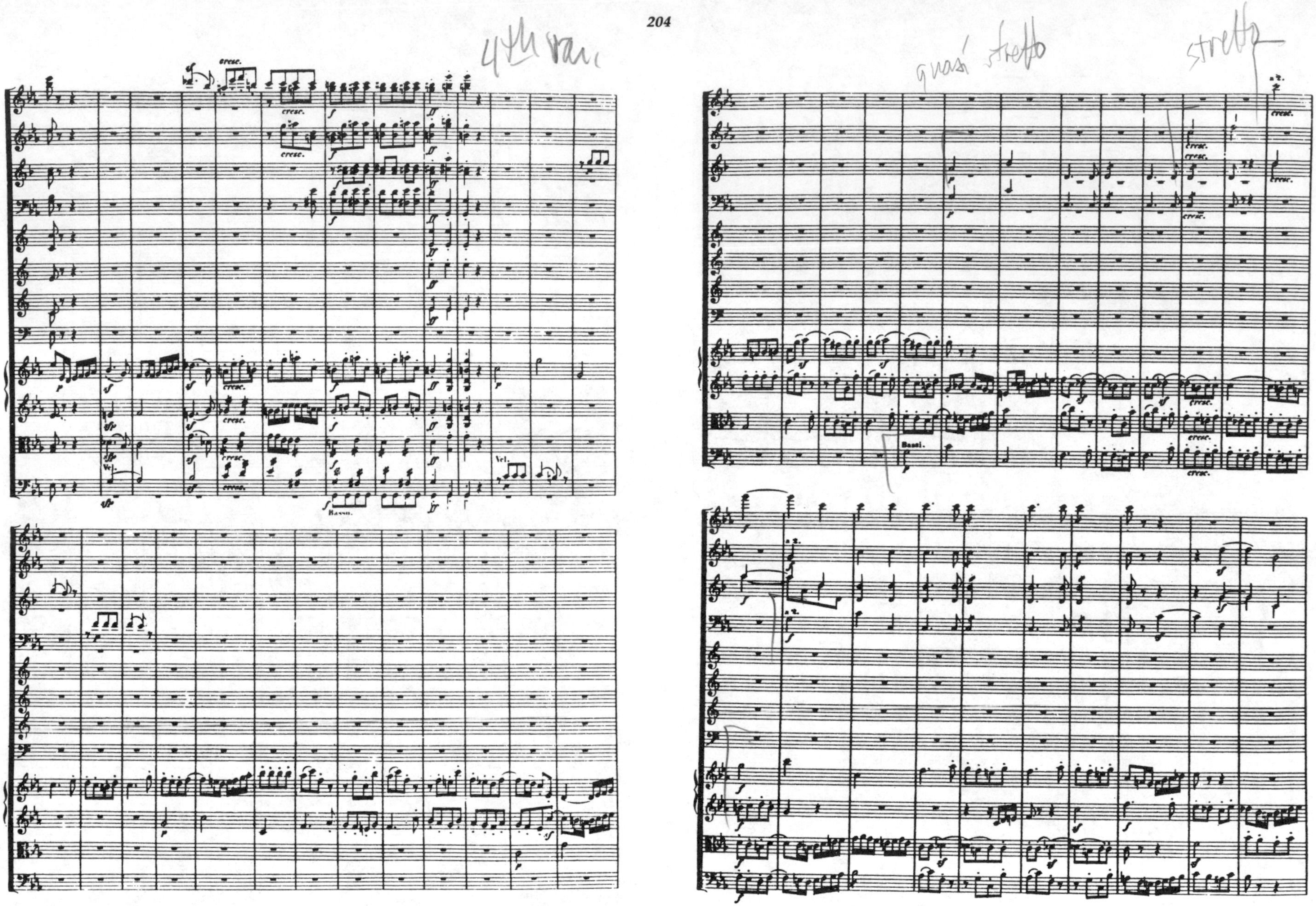
4th var.
quasi stretto
stretto
cresc.
Vcl.
Basso.
Bassi.

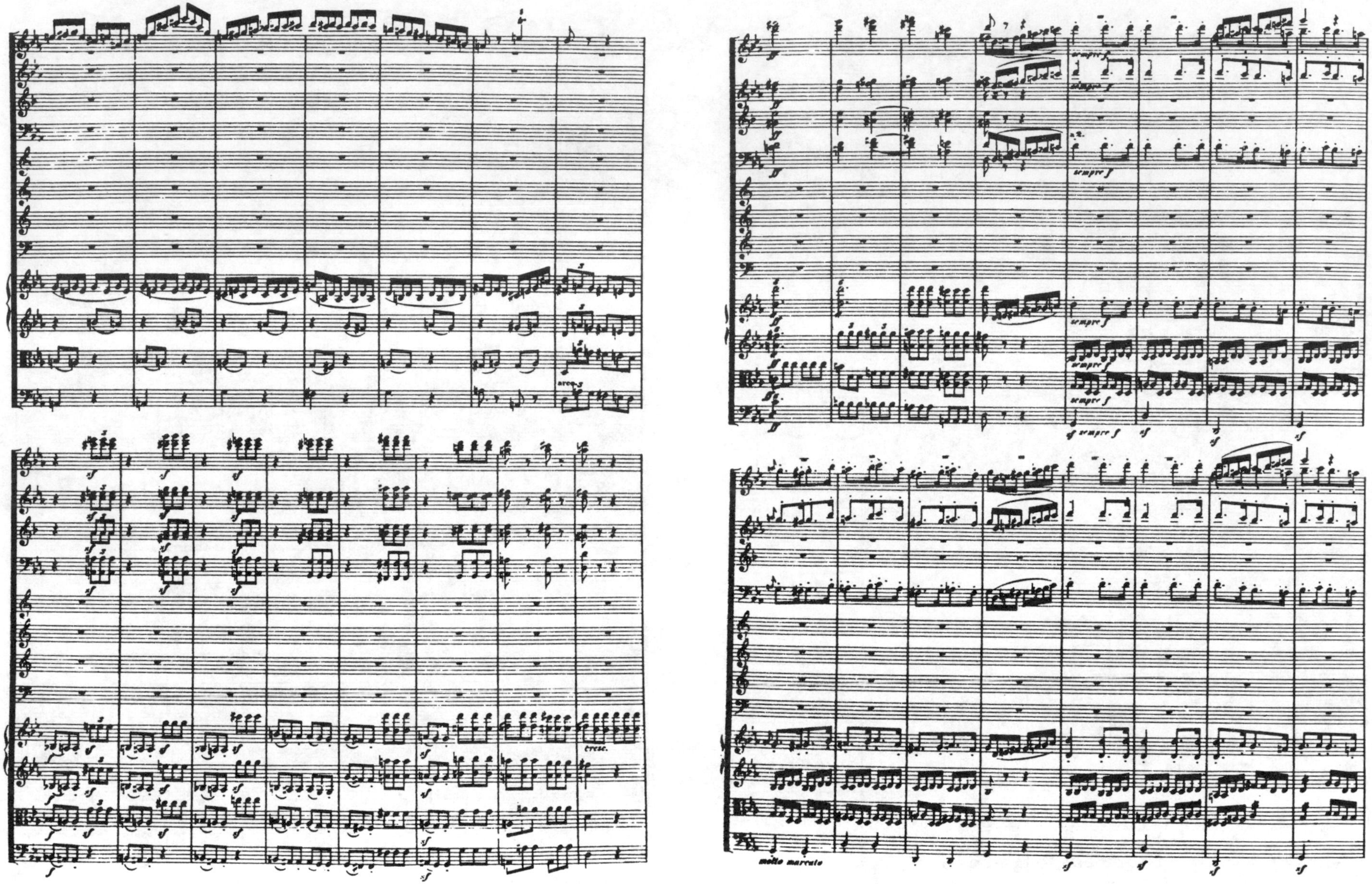
arco
cresc.
sempre f
a 2.
molto marcato

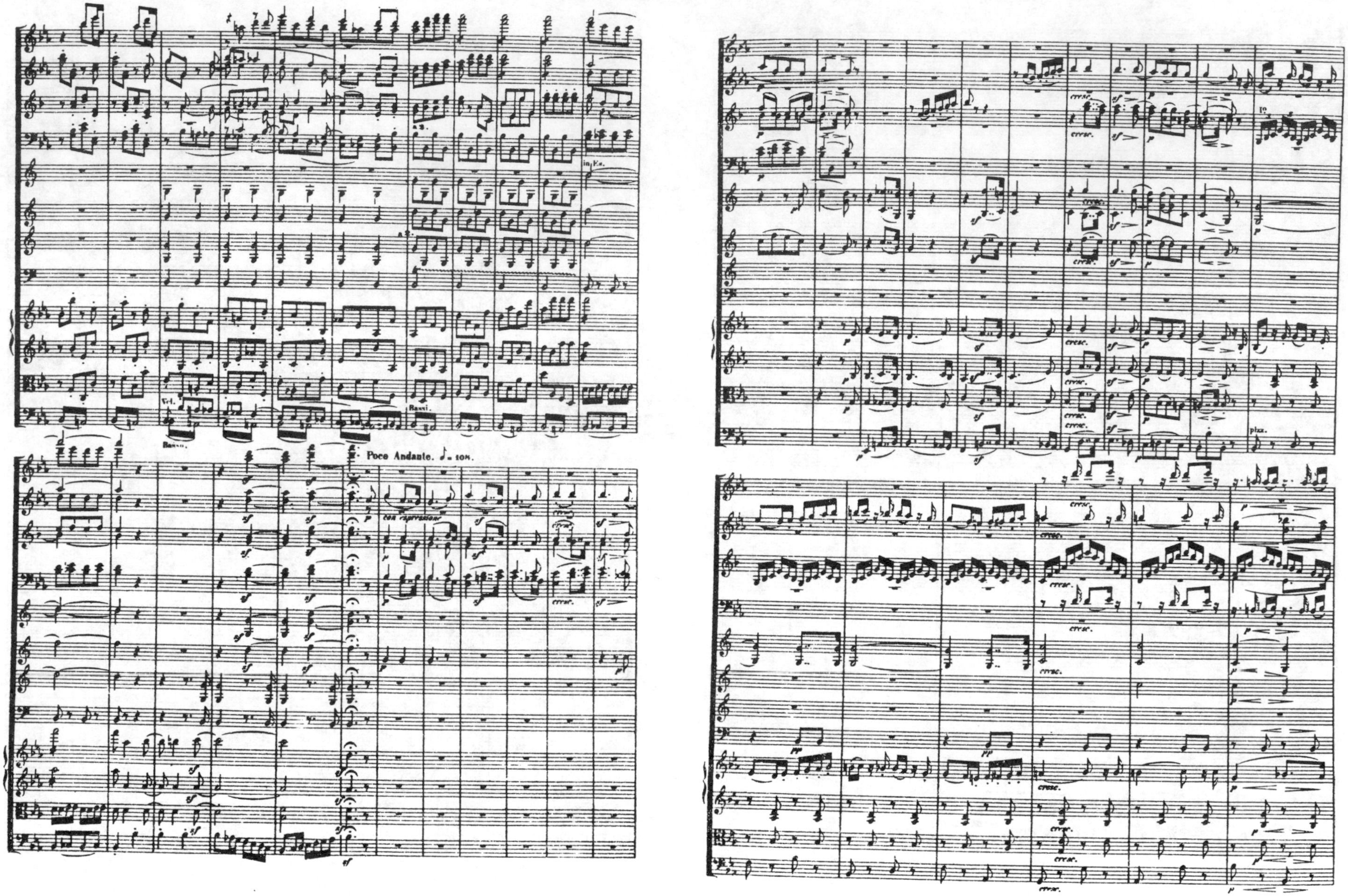

Vcl.
Bassi
a 2.
Poco Andante.
con espressione
cresc.
pizz.

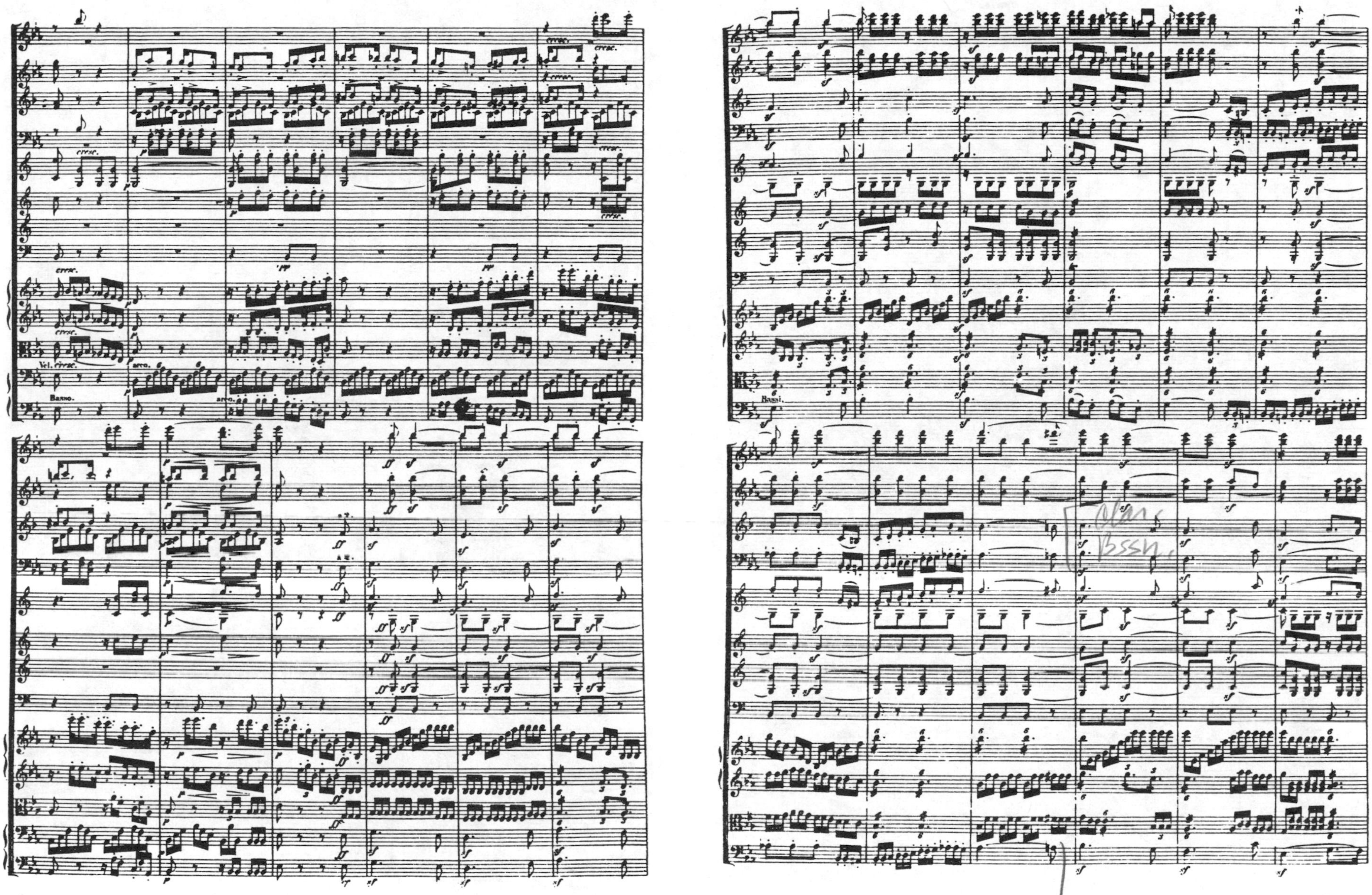

Contra Th (II)
augm, in Hns, cellos,
basses,

Coda

172. DER FREISCHÜTZ, Act II, Scene 4 (Finale): The Wolf Glen
Karl Maria von Weber (1786–1826)

Source: Dover Publications, Inc., Mineola, N.Y.

216

Anmerkung. Die folgenden beiden **bis** kommen in Anwendung im Fall Max nicht genug Zeit haben sollte.

Caspar (wirft ihm die Jagdflasche zu, die Max weglegt). Zuerst trink' einmal! Die Nachtluft ist kühl und feucht. Willst du selbst giessen?

Max. Nein, das ist wider die Abrede.

Caspar. Nicht? So bleib' ausser dem Kreise, sonst kostet's dein Leben!

Max. Was hab' ich zu thun. Hexenmeister?

Caspar. Fasse Muth! Was du auch hören und sehen magst, verhalte dich ruhig. (Mit eigenem heimlichen Grausen.) Käme vielleicht ein Unbekannter, uns zu helfen, was kümmert's dich? Kommt was anders, was thut's? — So etwas sieht ein Gescheidter gar nicht! O, wie wird das enden!

Caspar. Umsonst ist der Tod! Nicht ohne Widerstand schenken verborgene Naturen den Sterblichen ihre Schätze. Nur wenn du mich selbst zittern siehst, dann komme mir zu Hülfe und rufe, was ich rufen werde, sonst sind wir beide verloren.

Max. (macht eine Bewegung des Einwurfs.)

Caspar. Still! Die Augenblicke sind kostbar! (Der Mond ist bis auf einen schmalen Streif verfinstert. Caspar nimmt die Giesskelle.) Merk' auf, was ich hinein werfen werde, damit du die Kunst lernst! (Er nimmt die Ingredienzen aus der Jagdtasche und wirft sie nach und nach hinein.)

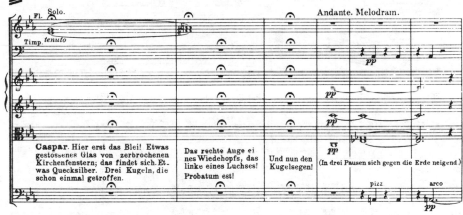

Caspar (höhnisch für sich). ich denke wohl auch.

Max (heftig zu Caspar). Hier bin ich, was hab' ich zu thun?

Caspar. Hier erst das Blei! Etwas gestossenes Glas von zerbrochenen Kirchenfenstern; das findet sich. Etwas Quecksilber. Drei Kugeln, die schon einmal getroffen.

Das rechte Auge eines Wiedehopfs, das linke eines Luchses! Probatum est!

Und nun den Kugelsegen!

(In drei Pausen sich gegen die Erde neigend.)

Caspar. Schütze, der im Dunkeln wacht, Samiel! Samiel! Hab'

acht, steh' mir bei in dieser

Nacht, bis der Zauber ist vollbracht. Salbe mir so Kraut als

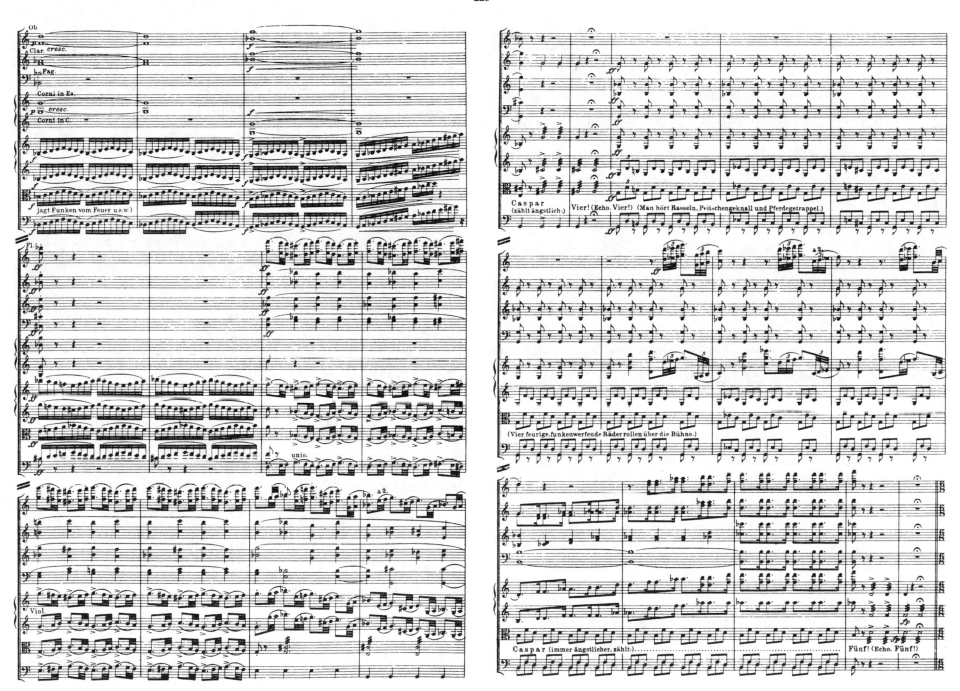

227

(Die Gewitter treffen furchtbar zusammen. Flammen schlagen aus der Erde. Irrlichter zeigen sich auf den Bergen u.s.w.)

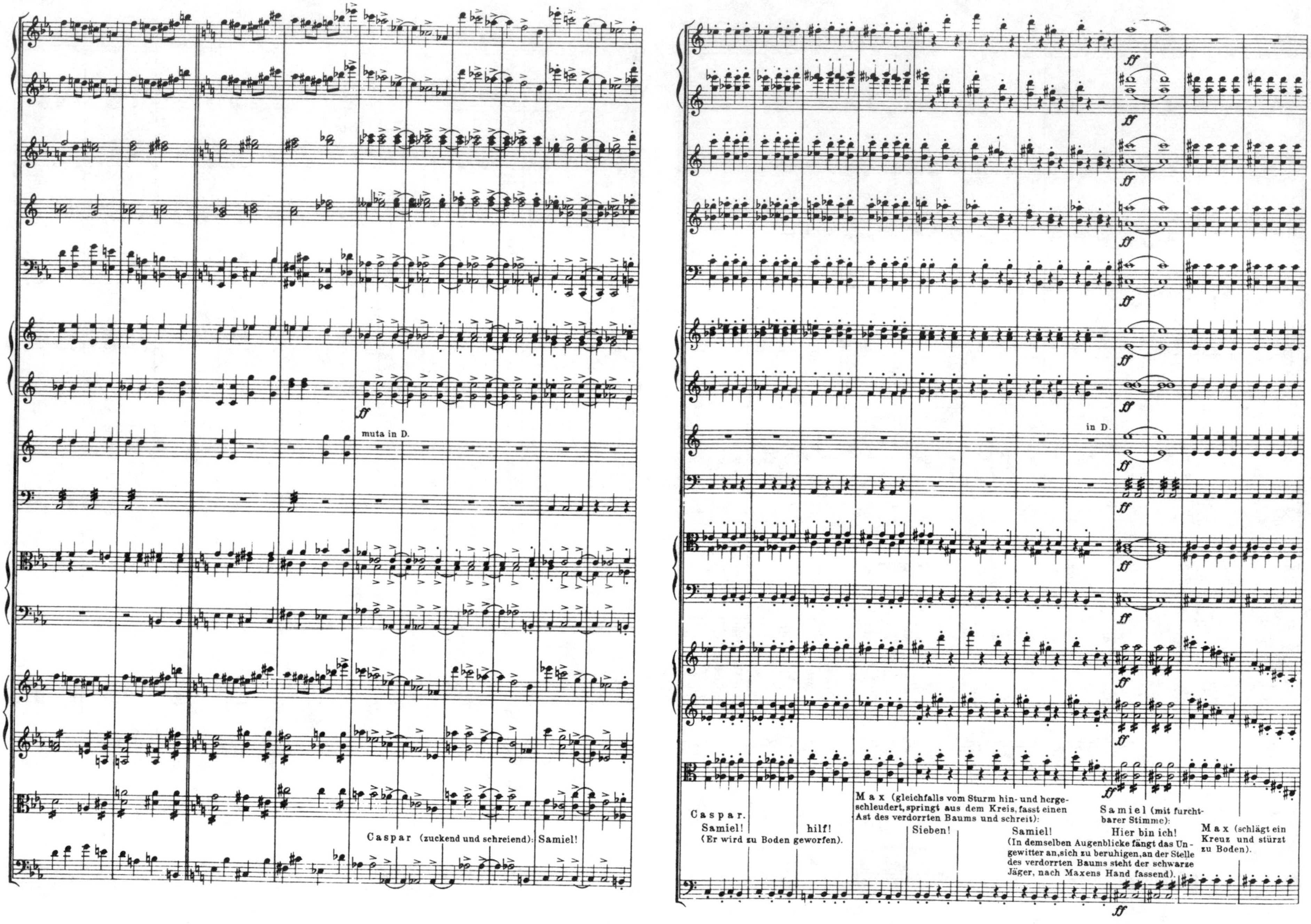

Caspar (zuckend und schreiend): Samiel!

Caspar.
Samiel! hilf!
(Er wird zu Boden geworfen).

Max (gleichfalls vom Sturm hin- und herge-
schleudert, springt aus dem Kreis, fasst einen
Ast des verdorrten Baums und schreit):

Sieben! Samiel!

Samiel (mit furcht-
barer Stimme):
Hier bin ich!
(In demselben Augenblicke fängt das Un-
gewitter an, sich zu beruhigen, an der Stelle
des verdorrten Baums steht der schwarze
Jäger, nach Maxens Hand fassend).

Max (schlägt ein
Kreuz und stürzt
zu Boden).

Setting is a dismal wooded glen with gnarled trees and crags. Caspar is making a circle with black boulders.

CHORUS OF SPIRITS:
Upper voices sing: Uhui! Uhui!
  (repeatedly)
Basses:
Milch des Mondes fiel auf's Kraut,
Spinnweb' ist mit Blut betaut!
Eh' noch wieder Abend graut,
Ist sie tot, die zarte Braut!
Eh' noch wieder sinkt die Nacht,
Ist das Opfer dargebracht.
(Die Uhr schlägt ganz in der Ferne 12.
  Der Kreis von Steinen ist vollendet.)
(Caspar reisst heftig den Hirschfänger
  heraus und stösst ihn mitten in den
  Todtenschädel.)
CASPAR (Erhebt den Hirschfänger mit
  dem Todtenkopfe, dreht sich dreimal
  herum u. ruft:)
Samiel! Samiel! erschien'!
Bei des Zaub'rers Hirngebein!
Samiel! Samiel! erschien'!

[NOTE: SAMIEL DOES NOT SING.]

SAMIEL:
Was rufst du mich?
  (Samiel tritt aus einem Felsen.)

CASPAR: (wirst sich nieder)
Du weisst, dass meine Frist schier
  abgelaufen ist.

SAMIEL:
Morgen!

CASPAR:
Verlang're sie noch einmal mir;

SAMIEL:
Nein!

CHORUS OF SPIRITS:
Upper voices: Uhui! Uhui!

Basses:
Milk of the moon fell on plant,
Spiderweb is bedewed with blood!
Before evening darkens again,
she will be dead, the dainty bride!
Before night falls again,
the sacrifice will be offered.
(In the distance a clock strikes 12. The
  circle of stones is complete.)
(Caspar violently yanks out his hunting
  knife and shoves it into the middle of
  a skull.)
CASPAR (raises the hunting knife with
  the skull, turns around three times
  and shouts:)
Samiel! Samiel! appear!
By the sorcerer's skull!
Samiel! Samiel! appear!

SAMIEL:
Why do you call me?
  (Samiel steps out from behind a
  rock.)

CASPAR: (in a lower voice)
You know that my time has almost run
  out.

SAMIEL:
Tomorrow!

CASPAR:
Extend it for me once more;

SAMIEL:
No!

CASPAR:
Ich bringe neue Opfer dir,

SAMIEL:
Welche?

CASPAR:
Mein Jagdgesell, er naht,
Er, der noch nie dein dunkles Reich
   betrat.

SAMIEL:
Was sein Begehr?

CASPAR:
Freikugeln sind's, auf die er Hoffnung
   baut.

SAMIEL:
Sechse treffen! Sieben äffen!

CASPAR:
Die siebente sei dein; aus seinem Rohr
   lenk' sie nach seiner Braut!
Dies wird ihn der Verzweiflung weih'n,
   ihn . . . und den Vater.

SAMIEL:
Noch hab' ich keinen Theil an ihr!

CASPAR:
Genügt er dir allein?

SAMIEL:
Das findet sich!

CASPAR:
Doch schenkst du Frist, und wieder auf
   drei Jahr', bring ich ihn dir zur Beute
   dar?!

SAMIEL:
Es sei! bei den Pforten der Hölle!
Morgen er oder du!
   (Verschwindet indet unter dumpfen
   Donner.)

CASPAR:
I bring you a new victim,

SAMIEL:
Who?

CASPAR:
My hunting companion, he approaches,
he, who has never yet set foot in your
   dark realm.

SAMIEL:
What [is] his desire?

CASPAR:
It is free-shooting bullets, on which he
   builds [his] hope.

SAMIEL:
Six hit [the mark]! Seven mocks!

CASPAR:
The seventh be yours; from his gun
   direct it toward his bride!
This will doom him to despair, him . . .
   and [her] father.

SAMIEL:
As yet I have no share in her!

CASPAR:
Is he alone sufficient for you?

SAMIEL:
That may be! [or, We'll find out!]

CASPAR:
However, you grant [me] time, and for
   another three years, [and] I will
   bring him to you as booty?!

SAMIEL:
So be it! by the gates of Hell! Tomorrow
   him or you!
   (He disappears under hollow
   thunder.)

(CASPAR: richtet sich langsam und
   erschopft auf und trocknet sich von
   der Stirn. Der Hirschfänger mit dem
   Todtenkopf ist verschwunden; an
   dessen Stelle ist ein kleiner Heerd
   mit glimmenden Kohlen aus der Erde
   gekommen.)

CASPAR: (sie erblickend)
Trefflich bedient!
   (thut einen Zug aus der Jagdflasche.)

Gesegn'es, Samiel!
   (trinkt)
Er hat mir warm gemacht!
Aber wo bleibt Max? Sollte er
   wortbrüchig werden? Samiel, hilf!

(Caspar geht, nicht ohne Beängstigund,
   im Kreise hin und her. Die Kohlen
   drohen zu verlöschen, er Kniet zu
   ihnen nieder, legt Reiss auf und bläst
   an. Die Eule und andere Vögel heben
   dabei die Flügel, als wollten sie
   anfachen.)

(Das Feuer raucht und knistert.)
(Max wird auf einer Felsenspitze, dem
   Wasserfall gegenuber sichtbar und
   beugt sich in die Schlucht herab.)

MAX:
Ha! Furchtbar gähnt der düst're
   Abgrund!
Welch' ein Grau'n, das Auge wähnt in
   einen Höllenpfuhl zu schau'n!
Wie dort sich Wetterwolken ballen;

der Mond verliert von seinem Schein;
gespenst'ge Nebelbilder wallen,

belebt ist das Gestein,
und hier . . . husch, husch!
fliegt Nachtgevögel auf im Busch!
Rothgraue, narb'ge Zweige strecken
nach mir die Riesenfaust!

(CASPAR rises slowly, totally
   exhausted, and wipes his forehead.
   The hunting knife with the skull has
   disappeared; in its place a small
   group with smouldering coals has
   come out of the earth.)

CASPAR: (noticing)
Excellent service!
   (He takes a drink from his hunting
   flask.)
Bless it, Samiel!
   (He drinks.)
He has made me [feel] warm!
But where is Max? Would he break his
   word? Samiel, help!

(Caspar goes, not without worry, around
   and around the circle. The coals
   threaten to go out, he kneels down by
   them, puts brush on them and blows
   on it. The owl and other birds take
   flight, as it flames.)

(The fire smokes and crackles.)
(Max appears on the edge of a crag
   above the waterfall and looks into the
   glen.)

MAX:
Ha! The gloomy abyss yawns fearfully!

What a horror! the eye imagines it is
   looking into a hellish pool!
How storm clouds are gathering over
   there;
the moon is losing its radiance;
ghostly mist-pictures are floating [in
   air],
the rock has come to life,
and here . . . whish! swish!
night birds fly in and out of the bushes!
Red-grey gnarled branches stretch
   their giant fists toward me!

Nein, ob das Herz auch graust—
ich muss! ich trotze allen Schrecken!
    (Er klettert einige Schritte herab.)

CASPAR: (erblickt ihn)
Dank Samiel! die Frist ist gewonnen!

CASPAR: (zu Max)
Kommst du endlich, Kamerad?
Ist das auch recht, mich so allein zu,
    lassen?
Siehst du nicht, wie mir's sauer wird?
    (Er hat das Feuer mit dem
    Adlerflügel angefacht und erhebt
    diesen im Gespräch gegen Max.)

MAX: (nach dem Adlerflügel starrend.)
Ich schoss den Adler aus hoher Luft;
ich kann nicht rückwärts, mein
    Schicksal ruft!
    (Er klettert einige Schritte, bleibt dann
    wieder stehen und blickt starr nach
    dem gegenüberstehenden Felsen.)

MAX:
Weh mir!

CASPAR:
So komm doch! Die Zeit eilt!

MAX:
Ich kann nicht hinab!

CASPAR:
Haasenherz! klimmst ja sonst wie eine
    Gemse!

MAX:
Sieh dort hin, sieh!
    (Er deutet nach dem Felsen; man
    erblickt eine weisse verschleierte
    Gestalt, die die Hände erhebt.)
Was dort sich weist, ist meiner Mutter
    Geist.
So lag sie im Sarg; so ruht sie im Grab.

No, although my heart shudders—
I must! I defy all terror!
    (He descends a few steps.)

CASPAR: (notices him)
Thanks, Samiel! The time is won! [or,
    More time was granted!]

CASPAR: (to Max)
Have you come at last, comrad?
Is it right to leave me so alone?

Do you not see how difficult it is for me?
    (He fanned the fire with an eagle's
    wing, and he raises it while speaking
    to Max.)

MAX: (staring at the eagle's wing)
I shot the eagle out of high air [at great
    height]; I cannot turn back, my
    destiny calls!
    (He descends a few steps, remains
    standing there, and stares fixedly at
    the rocks opposite him.)

MAX:
Woe is me!

CASPAR:
So come then! Time flies!

MAX:
I cannot go down!

CASPAR:
Coward! Once, you climbed like a
    chamois!

MAX:
Look over there, look!
    (He points to the rocks; one notices a
    white veiled figure with its hands
    upraised.)
What is seen there is my mother's ghost.

Thus she lay in her coffin; thus she rests
    in the grave.

Sie fleht mit warnendem Blick, sie winkt
    mir zurück!

CASPAR: (für sich)
Hilf Samiel!
(laut) Alberne Fratzen! Ha! Ha! Ha!
Sieh noch einmal hin, damit du die
    Folgen deiner feiger Thorheit
    erkennst'.

(Die verschleierte Gestalt ist
    verschwunden, man erblickt
    Agathens Gestalt mit aufgelösten
    Locken und wunderlich mit Laub
    und Stroh aufgeputzt. Sie gleicht
    einer Wahnsinnigen, und scheint in
    dem Begriff, sich in den Wasserfall
    hinab zu stürzen.)

MAX:
Agathe! Sie springt in den Fluss! Hinab!
    hinab! ich muss! Agathe! Sie springt
    in den Fluss! Agathe! hinab! ich
    muss! hinab! ich muss!
    (Die Gestalt verschwindet. Max klimmt
    vollends herab; der Mond fängt an
    sich zu verfinstern.)

CASPAR: (höhnisch für sich)
Ich denke wohl auch.

MAX: (heftig zu Caspar)
Hier bin ich, was hab ich zu thun?

CASPAR: (wirst ihm die Jagdflasche
    zu, die Max weglegt)
Zuerst trink' ein mal! Die Nachtluft ist
    kühl und feucht. Willst du selbst
    giessen?

MAX:
Nein, das ist wider die Abrede.

CASPAR:
Nicht? So blieb' ausser dem Kreise,
    sonst kostet's dein Leben!

She implores [me] with a warning
    glance; she waves me back.

CASPAR: (aside)
Help, Samiel!
(aloud) Foolish caricature! Ha! Ha! Ha!
Look again, you will realize the
    consequences of cowardly foolishness.

(The veiled figure has disappeared; one
    sees Agatha's figure with her hair
    mussed and dressed up with leaves
    and straw. She resembles a mad
    woman, and seems about to cast
    herself into the waterfall.)

MAX:
Agatha! She is leaping into the river!
    Down! Down! I must! Agatha! She is
    leaping into the river! Agatha! Down!
    I must! (repeated)
    (The figure disappears. Max descends;
    the moon begins to darken.)

CASPAR: (sneering; aside)
I should think so!

MAX: (vehemently, to Caspar)
Here I am; what must I do?

CASPAR: (throws him the hunting
    flask, which Max lays aside)
First drink a bit! The night air is cool
    and damp. Will you do the casting
    yourself?

MAX:
No, that is against the agreement.

CASPAR:
No? Then stay outside the circle;
    otherwise it costs your life!

MAX:
Was hab' ich zu thun, Hexenmeister?

CASPAR:
Fasse Muth! Was du auch hören und sehen magst, verhalte dich ruhig. (Mit eigenem heimlichen Grausen.) Käme vielleicht ein Unbekannter, uns zu helfen, was kummert's dich? Kommt was anders, was thut's?—So etwas sieht ein Gescheidter gar nicht!

MAX:
O, wie wird das enden!

CASPAR:
Umsonst is der Tod! Nicht ohne Widerstand schenken verborgene Naturen den Sterblichen ihre Schätze. Nur wenn du mich selbst zittern siehst, dann komme mir zu Hülfe und rufe, was ich rufen werde, sonst sind wir beide verloren.

MAX: (macht ein Bewegung des Einwurfs)

CASPAR:
Still! Die Augenblicke sind kostbar!

(Der Mond ist bis auf einen schmalen Streif verfinstert. Caspar nimmt die Giesskelle.)

Merk' auf, was ich hinein werfen werde, damit du die Kunst lernst! (Er nimmt die Ingredienzen aus der Jagdtasche und wirft sie nach und nach hinein.)

CASPAR:
Hier erst das Blei! Etwas gestossenes Glas von zerbrochenen Kirchenfenstern; das findet sich.

MAX:
What must I do, sorcerer?

CASPAR:
Take courage! Whatever you may see and hear, remain calm. (With his own inner horror.) If, perhaps, a stranger came to help us, what do you care? or, if anything else comes, what does it matter?—A clever man sees nothing like that!

MAX:
Oh, how will it end?!

CASPAR:
Death is free! Not without a struggle do hidden forces of nature yield their treasures to mortals. Only when you see me trembling, then come to help me, and call out what I call out; otherwise we are both lost.

MAX: (makes a gesture of objection)

CASPAR:
Quiet! Moments are precious!

(The moon is reduced to a small strip. Caspar takes the casting ladle.)

Pay attention to what I do, so you learn the art! (He takes the ingredients out of the hunting pouch and throws them in one after another.

CASPAR:
Here first the lead! Some shattered glass from broken church windows; we'll see. Some quicksilver. Three bullets

Etwas Quecksilber. Drei Kugeln, die schon einmal getroffen. Das rechte Auge eines Wiedehopfs, das linke eines Luchses!
Probatum est!
Und nun den Kugelsegen!
(In drei Pausen sich gegen die Erde neigend.)

CASPAR:
Schütze, der im Dunkeln wacht, Samiel! Samiel! Hab' Acht, steh' mir bei in dieser Nacht, bis der Zauber ist vollbracht. Salbe mir so Kraut also Blei, segn' es Sieben, Neun, und Drei, dass die Kugel tüchtig sei! Samiel! Samiel! her bei!

(Die Masse in der Giesskelle fängt an zu gähren und zu zischen, und giebt einen grünlich weissen Schein. Eine Wolke läuft über den Mondstreif, dass die ganze Gegend nur noch von dem Herdfeuer, den Augen der Eule und dem faulen Holze des Baumes beleuchtet ist.)

CASPAR (geisst, lässt die Kugel aus der Form fallen, und ruft):

CASPAR:	ECHO:
Eins!	Eins!
Zwei!	Zwei!

(Ein schwarzer Eber rauschelt durch's Gebüsch und jagt wild vorüber.)

| Drei! | Drei! |

(Ein Sturm erhebt sich beugt und bricht Wipfel der Bäume jagt Funken vom Feuer, u.s.w.)

that already have hit the mark. The right eye of a hoopoe, the left eye of a lynx.

It is proven!
And now the blessing of bullets!
(He bows to the earth three times.)

CASPAR:
Marksman, who keeps watch in darkness, Samiel! Samiel! Hear me! Stay by me this night, until the magic spell is completed. Anoint for me both herb and lead, bless it seven, nine, and three times, so that the bullets may be sound! Samiel! Come here!
(The mass in the crucible begins to ferment and hiss, and gives off a greenish light. A cloud passes over the moonstreak, so that the entire glen is illuminated by only the fire, and the owl's eyes and the rotting wood of the trees are seen in the light.)

CASPAR (casts, and as the bullets fall one by one from the mold, cries out):

CASPAR:	ECHO:
One!	One!
Two!	Two!

(A black boar rustles through the bushes and runs past wildly.)

| Three! | Three! |

(A storm gathers, and bends and breaks the top of the tree, and drives sparks from the fire, etc.)

Vier!   Vier!

(Man hört Rasseln, Peitschengeknall
    und Pferdegetrappel.)

Funf!   Funf!

MALE CHORUS:
Durch Berg und Thal, durch Schlund
    und Schacht, durch Thau und
    Wolken, Sturm und Nacht, durch
    Thau und Wolken, Sturm und Nacht!
Durch Höhle, Sumpf und Erdenkluft,
    durch Feuer, Erde, See, und Luft!
Joho! wau wau, joho, wau wau, joho! ho!
    ho! (repeated several times)

CASPAR:
Woho, das wilde Heer!
Sechs! woho!
       ECHO: Sechs! woho!

(Der ganze Himmel wird schwarze
    Nacht.)
(Die Gewitter treffen furchtbar
    zusammen. Flammen schlagen aus
    der Erde. Irrlichter zeigen sich auf
    den Bergen, u.s.w.)

CASPAR: (ruckend und schreiend)

Samiel! Samiel! Hilf!
    (Er wirdzu Boden geworfen.)

Four!   Four!

(One hears rustling, the crack of a whip,
    horses clattering around.)

Five!   Five!

MALE CHORUS:
Through mountain and vale, through
    gorge and ravine, through mist and
    cloud, storm and night, through mist
    and cloud, storm and night!
Through cave, swamp, and chasm,
    through fire, earth, sea, and air!
Yoho! wow, wow, yoho, wow, wow, yoho,
    ho! ho! (etc.)

CASPAR:
Woho! the wild host!
Six! woho!
       ECHO: Six! woho!

(The entire heavens becomes black
    night.)
(The storm strikes together with terror.
    Flames shoot out of the earth. Will-
    o'-the-wisps show themselves on the
    mountain, etc.)

CASPAR: (moving back and crying
    out):
Samiel! Samiel! Help!
    (He throws himself to the ground.)

MAX:
(gleichfalls von Sturm hin- und
    hergeschleudert, springt aus dem
    Kreis, fasst einen Ast des verdorrten
    Baums und Schreit):
Sieben!   Samiel!

SAMIEL: (mit furchtbarer Stimme):
Hier bin ich!

(In demselben Augenblicke fängt das
    Ungewitter an, sich zu beruhigen, an
    der Stelle des verdorrten Baums steht
    der schwarze Jäger, nach Maxens
    Hand fassend.)

MAX (schlägt ein Kreuz und sturzt zu
    Boden)
    (Es schlagt Eins.)
    (plotzliche Stille)

(Samiel ist verschwanden.)

(Caspar liegt noch mit dem Gesicht
    zu Boden.)

(Max richtet sich konvulsivisch auf.)

Der Vorhang fällt.

End das zweiten Actes.

MAX:
(as the storm hurls itself about, Max
    springs out of the circle, grasps a
    bough of the withered tree, and cries
    out):
Seven!   Samiel!

SAMIEL: (in a frightening voice):
Here am I!

(In the same instant the thunderstorm
    begins to lull, in the place of the
    withered tree stands the black
    hunter, grasping Max's hand.)

MAX (makes sign of the cross and falls
    to the ground)
    (The clock chimes One.)
    (sudden stillness)

(Samiel has disappeared.)

(Caspar still lies with his face to the
    ground.)

(Max stands up, convulsively.)

The curtain falls.

End of the second Act.

173. EDWARD, Ballad
Carl Loewe (1796–1869)

Source: Breitkopf & Härtel, Wiesbaden

Und was soll dei _ ne Mut-ter thun,

Mut _ _ _ _ ter! Mut _ _ _ _ ter!

Edward? Edward, und was soll dei _ ne Mut-ter thun, mein

der Fluch der Höl _ _ _ _ _ le soll

Sohn, mein Sohn, das sage mir? O! O! Der Fluch der

auf Euch ruhn, denn Ihr, Ihr riethet's mir! O!

Höl _ _ _ _ le soll auf Euch ruhn,

con Ped.

Original Scottish Ballad	Translated into German	Modern English
"Why dois your brand sae drap wi' bluid, Edward, Edward?" Why dois your brand sae drap wi' bluid? And why sae sad gang yee, O?"	Dein Schwert, wie ist's von Blut so roth, Edward! Edward, dein Schwert, wie ist's von Blut so roth, und gehst so traurig da? O!	Why is your sword so red with blood, Edward! Edward, your sword, why is it so red with blood, and why are you so sad? O!
"O, I hae killed my hauke sae guid, Mither, Mither, O, I hae killed my hauke sae guid, And I had nae mair bot hee, O."	Ich hab geschlagen meinen Geyer todt, Mutter! Mutter, ich hab geschlagen meinen Geyer todt, und das, das geht mir nah! O!	I have killed my hunting hawk, Mother! Mother, I have killed my hunting hawk, and that, that gives me none! O!
"Your haukis bluid was nevir sae reid, Edward, Edward, Your haukis bluid was nevir sae reid, My deir son I tell thee, O."	Deines Geyers Blut ist nicht so roth, Edward! Edward, deines Geyers Blut ist nicht so roth, mein Sohn, bekenn mir frei, O!	Your hunting hawk's blood is not so red, Edward! Edward, your hunting hawk's blood is not so red; my son, confess to me freely, O!
"O, I hae killed my reid-roan steid, Mither, Mither, O, I hae killed my reid-roan steid, That erst was sae fair und frie, O."	Ich hab geschlagen mein Rothross todt, Mutter! Mutter, ich hab geschlagen mein Rothross todt, 's war so stolz und treu. O!	I have killed my red horse, Mother! Mother, I have killed my red horse; it was so proud and faithful. O!
"Your steid was auld, and yee hae gat mair, Edward, Edward, Your Steid was auld, and yee hae gat mair, Sum other dule ye drie, O."	Dein Ross war alt und hast's nicht noth, Edward, Edward! Dein Ross war alt und hast's nicht noth, dich drückt andrer Schmerz. O!	Your horse was old and it is not needed, Edward, Edward! Your horse was old and it is not needed; other pain presses you. O!
"O, I hae killed my fadir deir, Mither, Mither, O, I hae killed my fadir deir, Alas, and wae is mee, O!"	Ich hab geschlagen meinen Vater todt! Mutter! Mutter, ich hab geschlagen meinen Vater todt, und das, das quält mein Herz. O!	I have killed my father! Mother! Mother, I have killed my father, and that, that torments my heart. O!
"And whatten penance wul yee drie for that, Edward, Edward? And whatten penance wul yee drie for that? My deir son, now tell me, O."	Und was wirst du nun an dir thun, Edward? Edward, und was wirst du nun an dir thun? mein Sohn, das sage mir! O!	And what will you do with yourself now, Edward? Edward, and what will you do with yourself now? my son, tell me that! O!

brand = sword
sae = so
hauke = hawk; haukis = hawk's

dule = grief
gang = go
drie = endure

"Ile set my feit in yonder boat, Mither,
  Mither,
Ile set my feit in yonder boat,
And Ile fare ovir the sea, O."

"And what wul yee doe wi' your towirs
  and your ha', Edward, Edward?
And what wul yee doe wi' your towirs
  and your ha',
That were sae fair to see, O?"

"Ile let thame stand tul they doun fa',
  Mither, Mither,
Ile let thame stand tul they doun fa',
For here nevir mair maun I bee, O."

"And what wul yee leive to your bairns
  and your wife, Edward, Edward?
And what wul yee leive to your bairns
  and your wife,
When yee gang ovir the sea, O?"

"The warld is room, late them beg thrae
  life, Mither, Mither,
The warld is room, late them beg thrae
  life,
For thame nevir mair wul I see, O."

"And what wul yee leive to your ain
  mither deir, Edward, Edward?
And what wul yee leive to your ain
  mither deir,
My deir son, now tell me, O."

"The curse of hell frae me sall yee beir,
  Mither, Mither,
The curse of hell frae me sall yee beir,
Sic counseils yee gave to me, O."

—Anonymous

sic = such
bairns = children
counseils = counsels
warld = world
thrae = through

Auf Erden soll mein Fuss nicht ruhn,
  Mutter, Mutter!
auf Erden soll mein Fuss nicht ruhn,
will wandern übers Meer! O!

Und was soll werden dein Hof und Hall,
  Edward?
Edward, und was soll werden dein Hof
  und Hall?
so herrlich sonst, so schön! O!

Ach, immer steh's und sink' und fall'!
  Mutter! Mutter!
Ach, immer steh's und sink' und fall',
ich werd' es nimmer sehn! O!

Und was soll werden aus Weib und
  Kind, Edward?
Edward, und was soll werden Weib und
  Kind,
wann du gehst übers Meer? O!

Die Welt ist gross, lass sie betteln drin,
  Mutter! Mutter!
die Welt ist gross, lass sie betteln drin,

ich, ich seh sie nimmermehr! O! O!

Und was soll deine Mutter thun,
  Edward?
Edward, und was soll deine Mutter
  thun,
mein Sohn, mein Sohn, das sage mir?
  O! O!

Der Fluch der Hölle soll auf Euch ruhn,
  Mutter! Mutter!
der Fluch der Hölle soll auf Euch ruhn,
denn Ihr, Ihr riethet's mir! O!

—Johann Gottfried Herder

My foot shall not rest on earth, Mother,
  Mother!
my foot shall not rest on earth,
[I] will wander over the sea! O!

And what will become of your courtyard
  and hall, Edward?
Edward, and what will become of your
  courtyard and hall?
so magnificent otherwise, so beautiful!
  O!

Ah, let them stand and decay and fall!
  Mother! Mother!
Ah, let them stand and decay and fall;
I will never see it! O!

And what will become of your wife and
  child, Edward?
Edward, and what will become of your
  wife and child,
when you go over the sea? O!

The world is big, let them beg therein,
  Mother! Mother!
the world is big, let them beg therein;

I, I will never see them again! O! O!

And what will your Mother do,
  Edward?
Edward, and what will your Mother do,

my son, my son, tell me that? O! O!

The curse of hell shall rest on you,
  Mother! Mother!
the curse of hell shall rest on you,
since you, you advised me to do it! O!

174. SYMPHONY NO. 8, in B Minor, ("Unfinished"), D. 759, mvt. 1
Franz P. Schubert (1797–1828)

Source: Breitkopf & Härtel, Wiesbaden

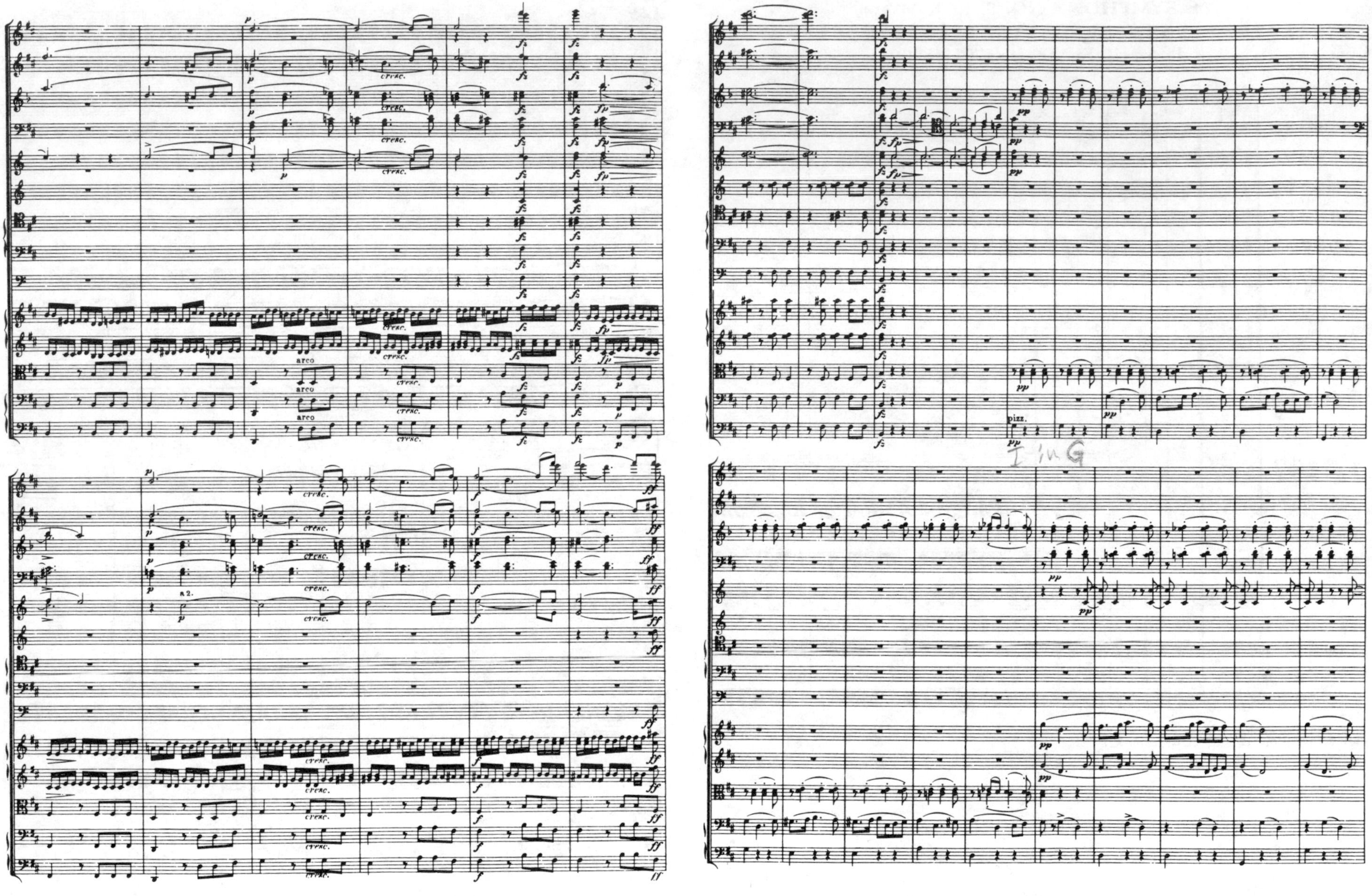
cresc.
arco
fz
fp
p
f
ff
pp
a 2.
pizz.
I in G

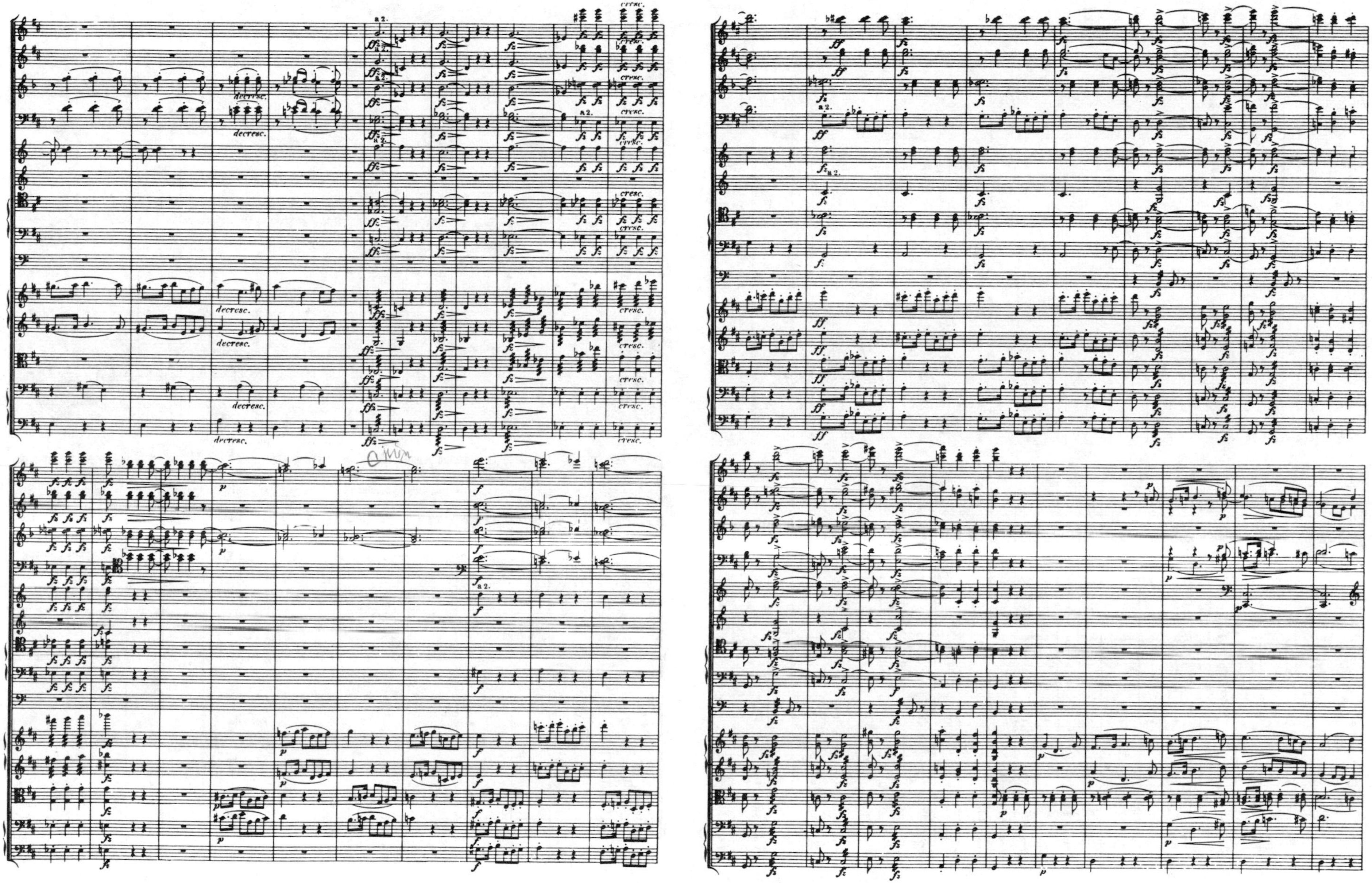
a 2.
decresc.
cresc.

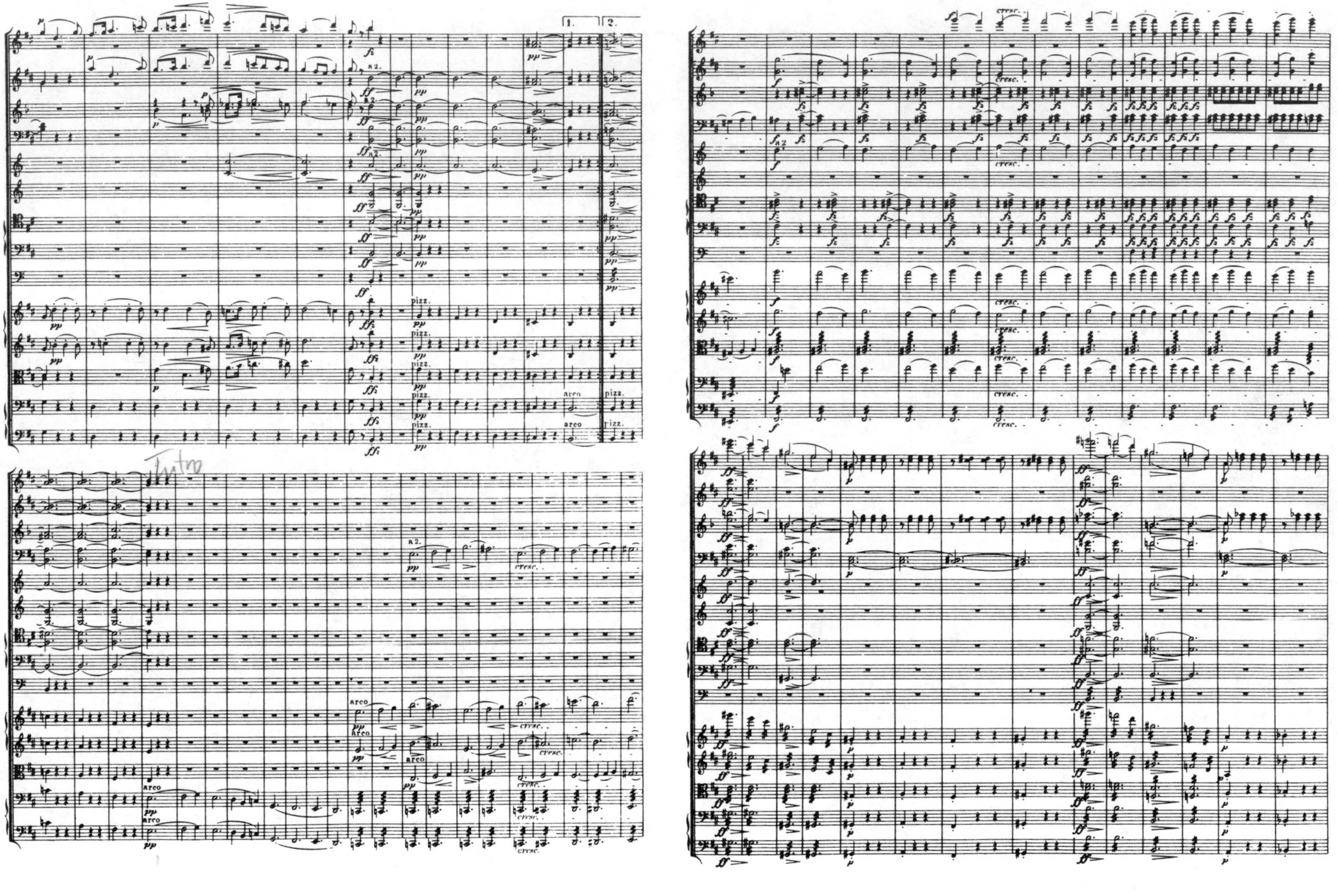

1.
2.
a 2.
pizz.
arco
cresc.
Tutti

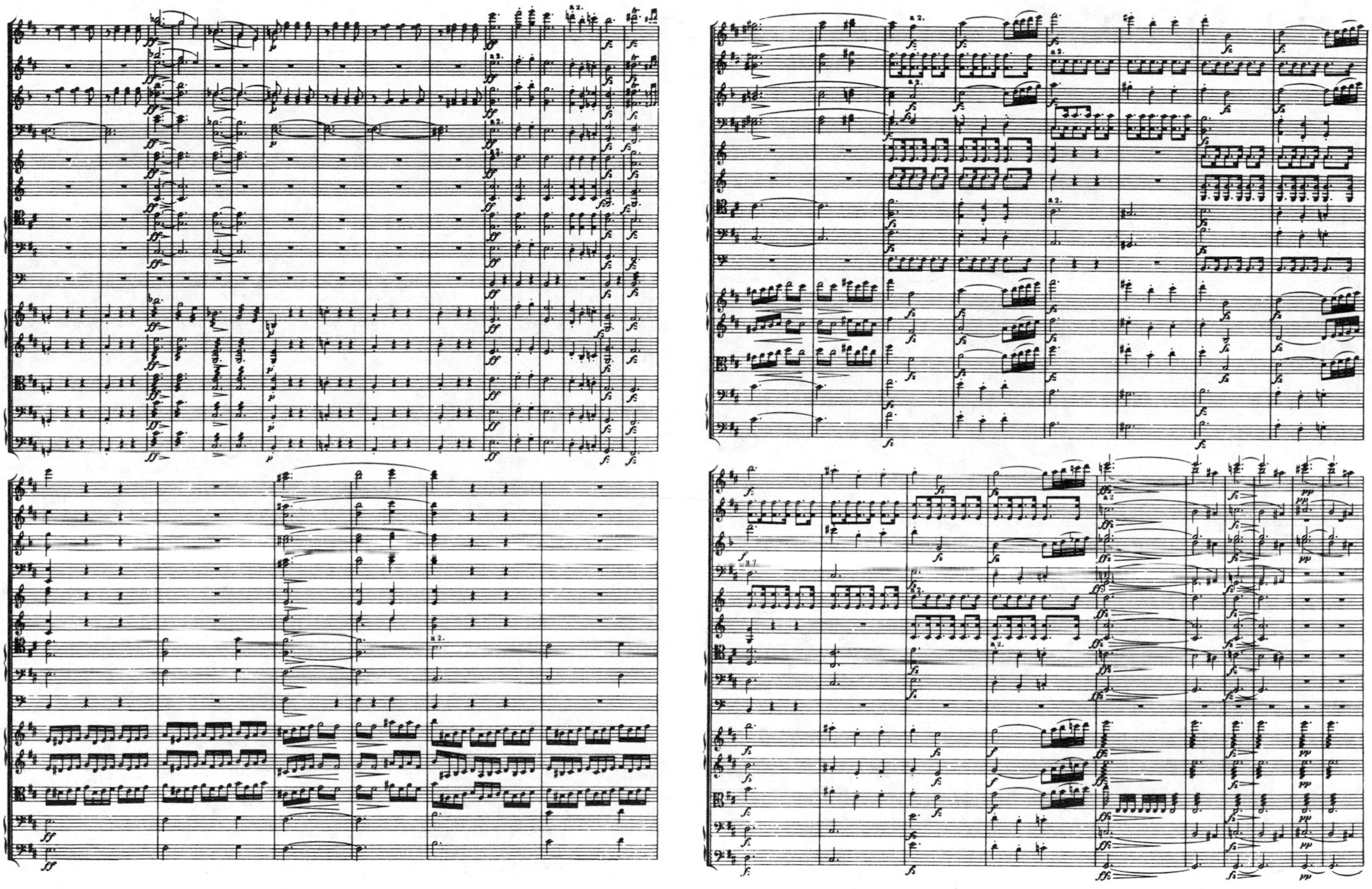
a 2.

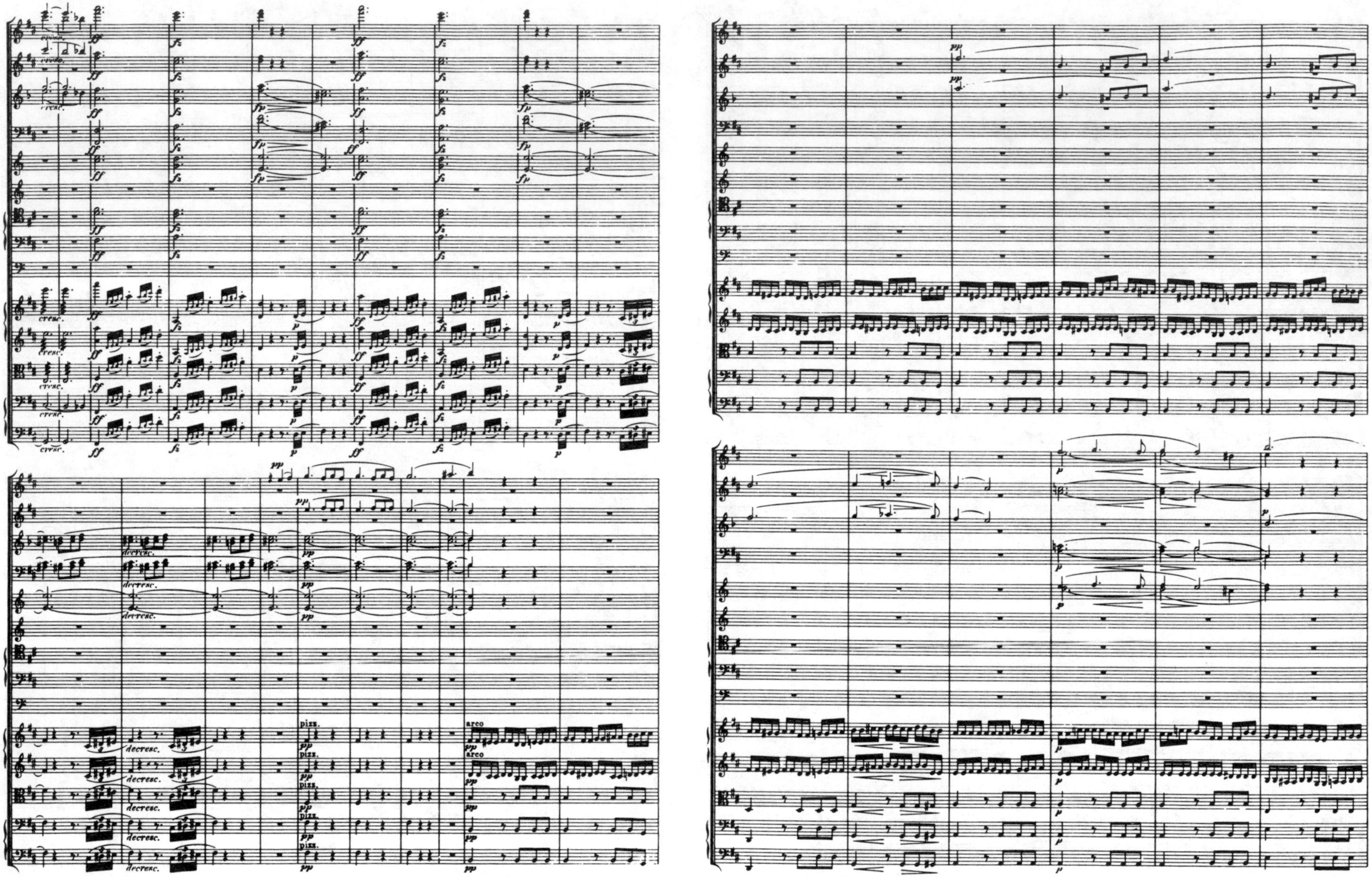
cresc.
ff
fz
fp
decresc.
pp
pizz.
arco
p

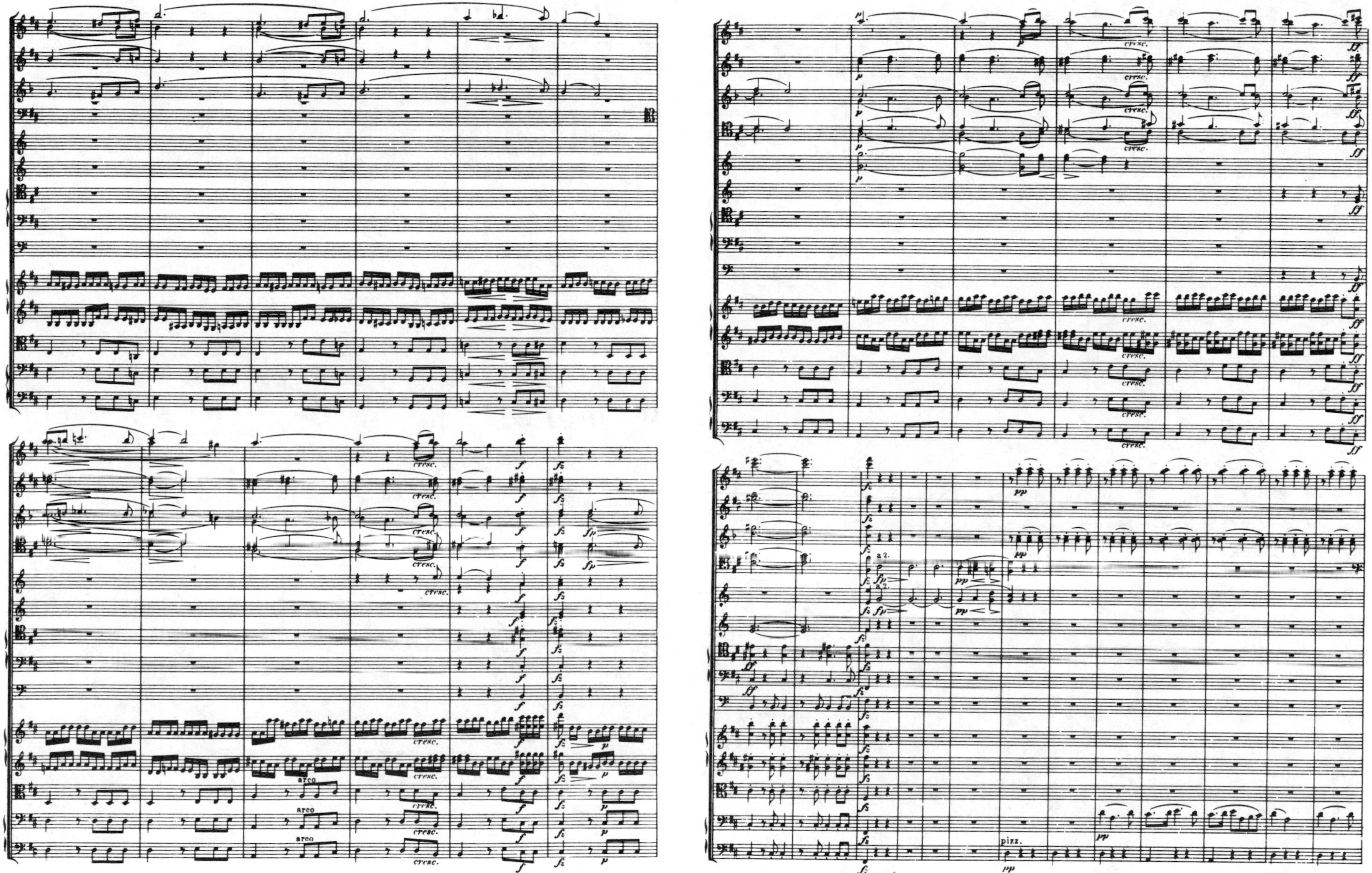

D

bi-focal

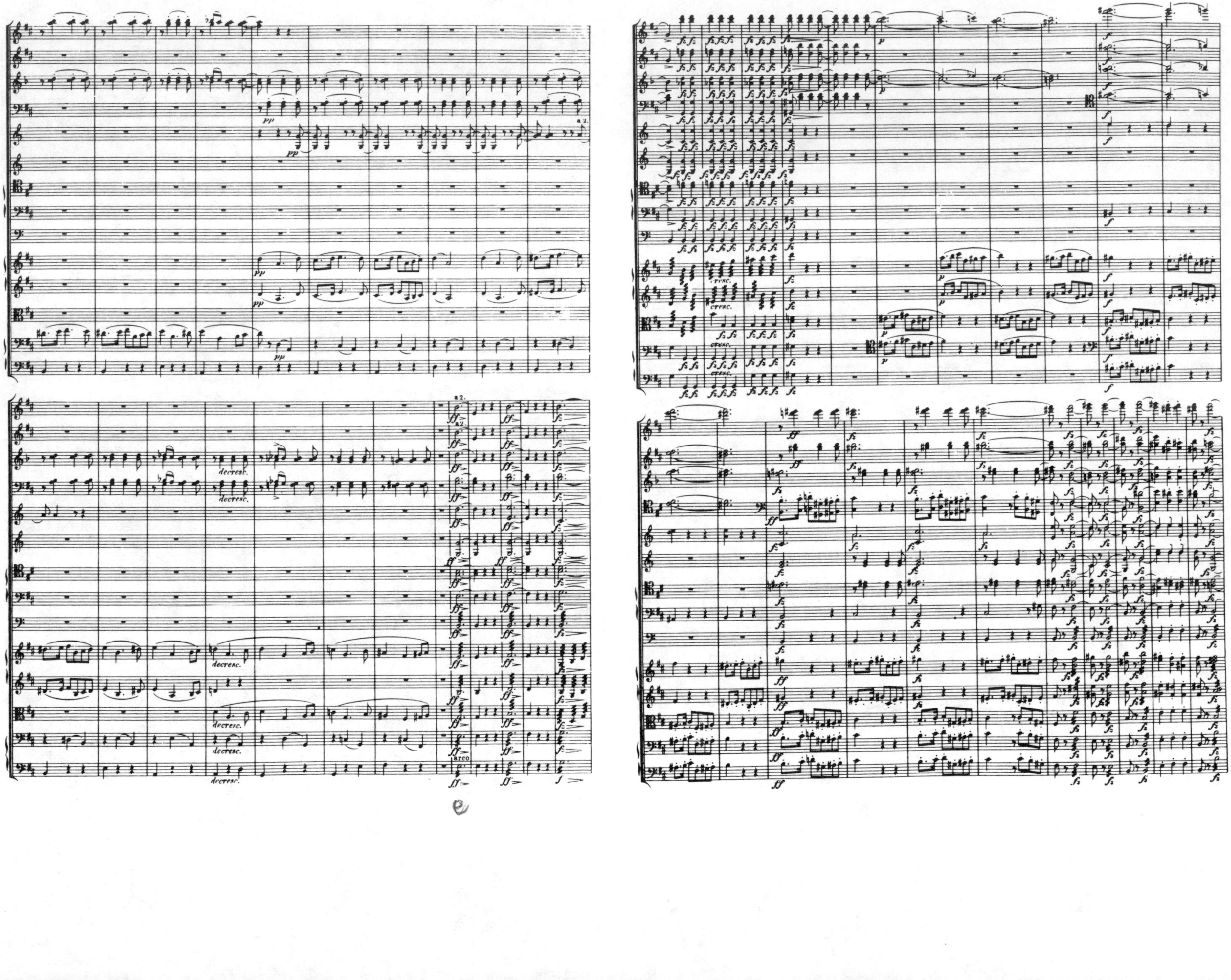
a 2.
pp
decresc.
cresc.
arco
ff
fz

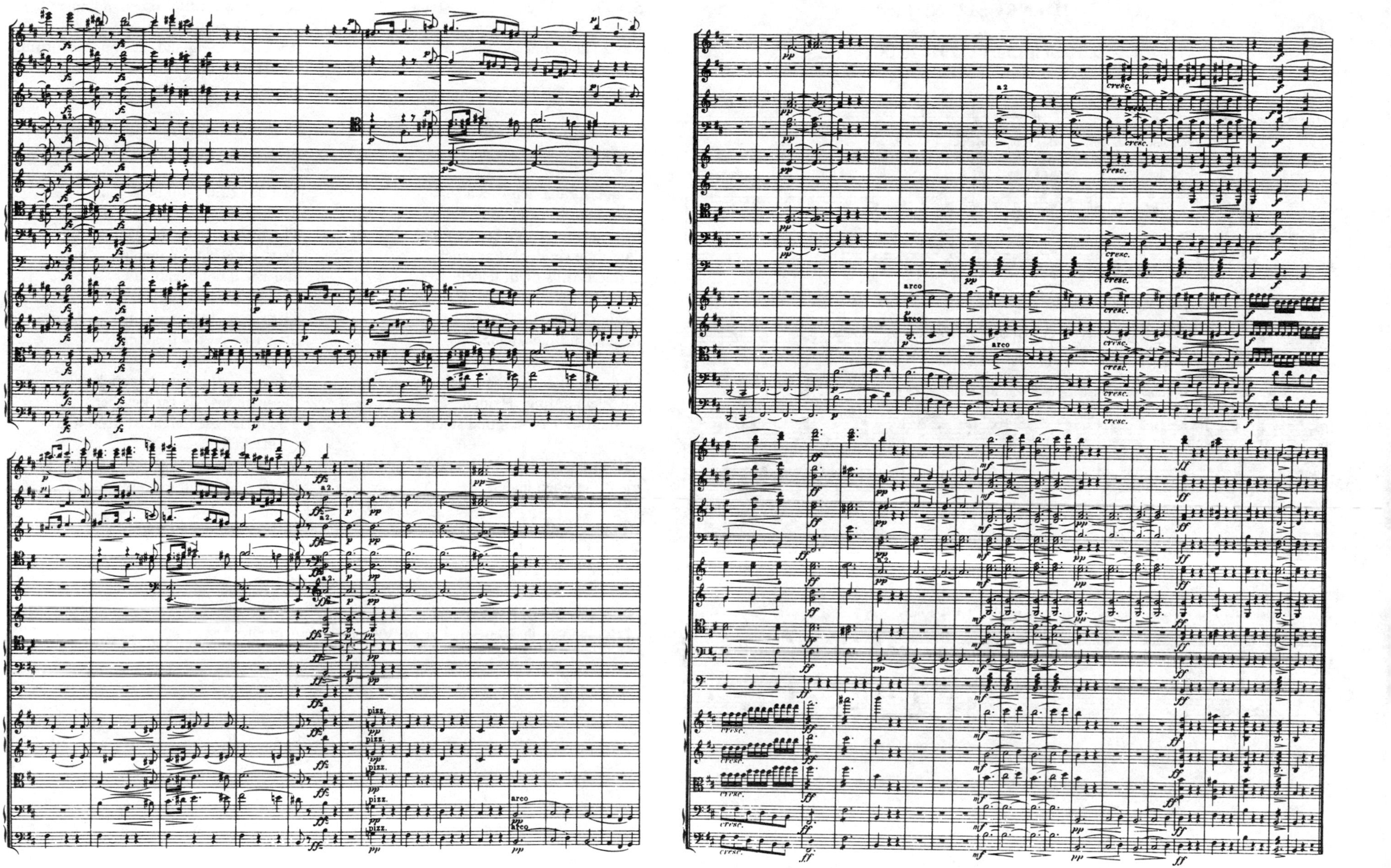
a 2.
pizz.
arco
cresc.
a 2

175. HEIDENRÖSLEIN, Lied

Franz P. Schubert (1797-1828)

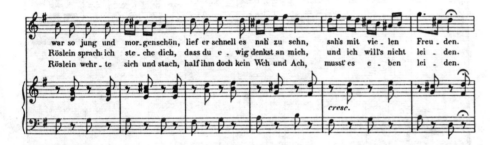

Source: Breitkopf & Härtel, Wiesbaden

Sah ein Knab' ein Röslein stehn,
Röslein auf der Heiden,
war so jung und morgenschön,
lief er schnell es nah' zu sehn,
sah's mit vielen Freuden.

Röslein, Röslein, Röslein rot,
Röslein auf der Heiden.

Knabe sprach: ich breche dich,
Röslein auf der Heiden.
Röslein sprach: ich steche dich,
dass du ewig denkst an mich,
und ich will's nicht leiden.

Röslein, Röslein, Röslein rot,
Röslein auf der Heiden.

Und der wilde Knabe brach
'sRöslein auf der Heiden.
Röslein wehrte sich und stach,

half ihm doch kein Weh und Ach,
musst' es eben leiden.

Röslein, Röslein, Röslein rot,
Röslein auf der Heiden.
—J. W. von Goethe

A boy saw a little rose standing,
little rose on the heather,
it was so young and morning-beautiful,
[that] he ran fast to see it close,*
viewed it with much pleasure.

Little rose, little rose, little red rose,
little rose on the heather.**

The boy said: "I'll pick you,
little rose on the heather."
The little rose spoke: "I'll prick you,
that you eternally remember me,
and I will not permit it.

Little rose, little rose, little red rose,
little rose on the heather.

And the impetuous boy picked it,
the little rose on the heather.
The little rose defended itself and
    pricked,
however, no wails of woe helped it;
it just had to suffer.

Little rose, little rose, little red rose,
little rose on the heather.

*up close, at close range.
**Heiden can be translated as heather, heath, or moor.

176. ERLKÖNIG, Lied
Franz P. Schubert (1797–1828)

Source: Breitkopf & Härtel, Wiesbaden

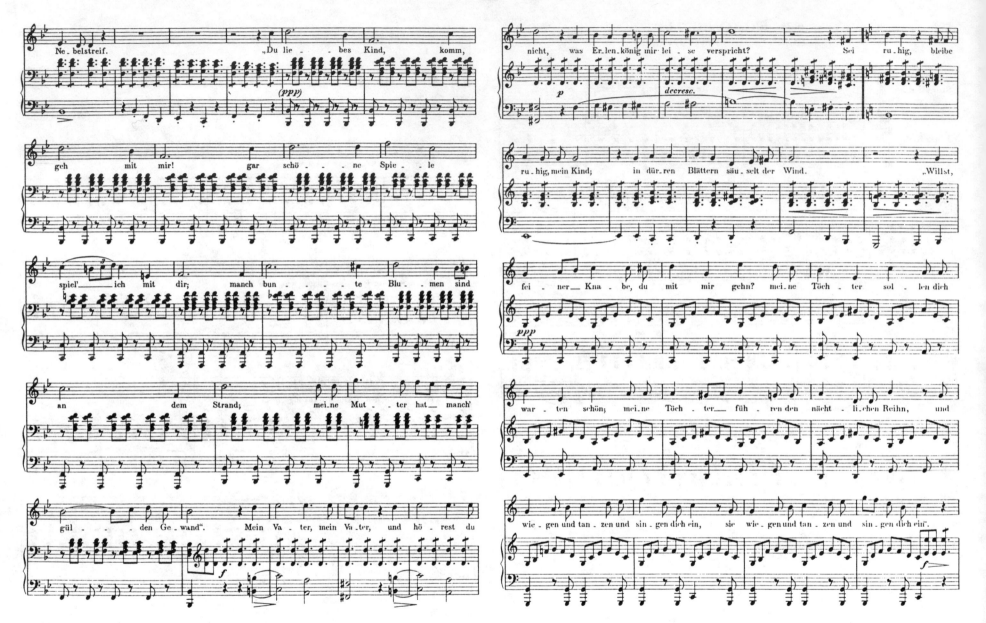

Wer reitet so spät durch Nacht und Wind?
Es ist der Vater mit seinem Kind;
er hat den Knaben wohl in dem Arm,
er fasst ihn sicher, er hält ihn warm.

Mein Sohn, was birgst du so bang dein besicht?
Siehst, Vater, du den Erlkönig nicht?
Den Erlkönig mit Kron' und Schweif?
Mein Sohn, es ist ein Nebelstreit.

"Du liebes Kind, komm, geh mit mir!
gar schöne Spiele spiel' ich mit dir;
manch' bunte Blumen sind an dem Strand;
meine Mutter hat manch' gülden Gewand."

Mein Vater, mein Vater, und hörest du nicht,
was Erlenkönig mir leise verspricht?
Sei ruhig, bleibe ruhig, mein Kind;
in dürren Blättern säuselt der Wind.

"Willst, feiner Knabe, du mit mir gehn?
mein Töchter sollen dich warten schön;
meine Töchter führen den nächtlichen Reihn
und wiegen und tanzen und singen dich ein."

Mein Vater, mein Vater, und siehst du nicht dort
Erlkönigs Töchter am düstern Ort?
Mein Sohn, mein Sohn, ich seh es genau,
es scheinen die alten Weiden so grau.

"Ich liebe dich, mich reizt deine schöne Gestalt;
und bist du nicht willig, so brauch' ich Gewalt."

Who rides so late through night and wind?
It is the father with his child;
he has the boy well in his arms,
he holds him securely, he keeps him warm.

"My son, why are you hiding your face so fearfully?"
"Father, don't you see the Erlking?
The Erlking with crown and train?"
"My son, it is a streak of mist."

"You dear child, come, go with me!
very nice games I'll play with you;
many multicolored flowers are on the shore;
my mother has many golden garments."

"My father, my father, and do you not hear
what the Erlking softly promises me?"
"Be quiet, remain quiet, my child;
the wind is rustling in dry leaves."

"My handsome boy, will you come with me?
my daughters shall take good care of you,
my daughters lead the nightly procession*
and shall cradle and dance and sing you to sleep."

"My father, my father, and don't you see there
The Erlking's daughters in [that] dark place?"
"My son, my son, I see it clearly,
the old willows are gleaming so grey."

"I love you, your beautiful figure fascinates me;
and if you are not willing, then I will use force."

Mein Vater, mein Vater, jetzt fasst er mich an!
Erlkönig hat mir ein Leids gethan.

Dem Vater grauset's, er reitet geschwind,
er hält in Armen das ächzende Kind,

erreicht den Hof mit Müh' und Noth;

in seinem Armen das Kind war tot.

—J. W. von Goethe

"My father, my father, now he is taking hold of me!
The Erlking has hurt me!"

The father shudders, he rides faster,

he holds in [his] arms the groaning child,
[he] reaches the courtyard exhausted and troubled;

in his arms the child was dead.

*probably, a procession dance

177. IMPROMPTU NO. 3 (D. 935)
Franz P. Schubert (1797–1828)

256

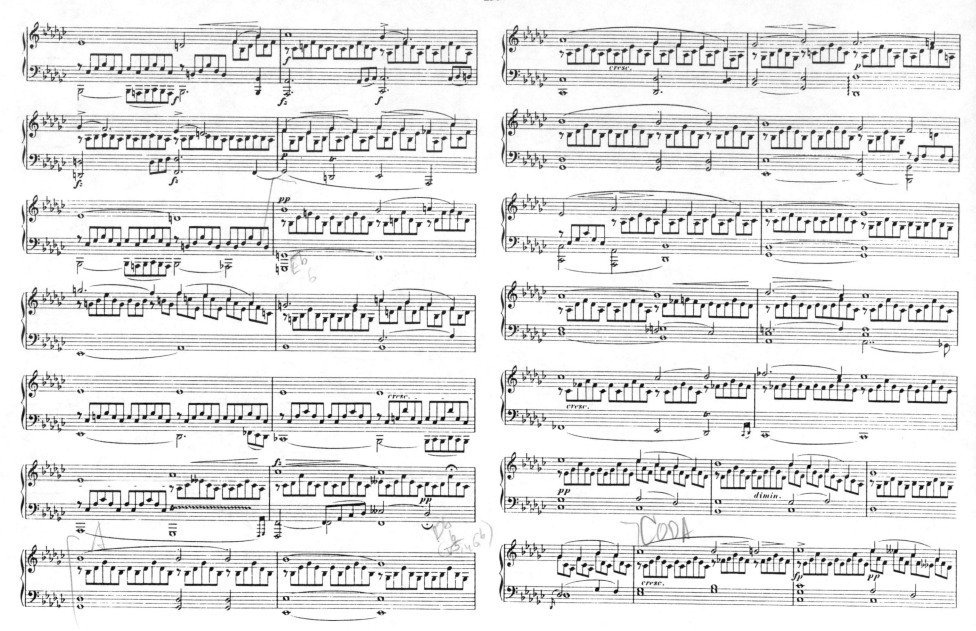

Harmonic reinterpretation of descending bass

178. HOFFNUNG, Lied
Luise Reichardt (1779-1826)

Simply and fervently, the 2nd stanza with rapt expression
(*Einfach und innig, die 2te Strophe mit dem Ausdruck der Verklärung*)

In the time of ro - ses, Hope, thou wear - y heart!
Wenn die Ro - sen blü - hen, hof - fe, lie - bes Herz;

Spring, a balm dis - clo - ses For the keen - est smart.
still und kühl ver - glü - hen wird der hei - sse Schmerz.

Tho' thy grief o'er - come thee, Thru the win - ter's gloom,
Wirp den Win - ter ü - ber oft un - heil - bar schien,

Thou shalt thrust it from thee, When the ro - ses bloom.
es ent - weicht das Fei - ber, Wenn die Ro - sen blüh'n.

Fieber

Source: *The Artistic Soprano*, M. Witmark & Sons, © 1913, New York, NY.

Wenn die Rosen blühen,
hoffe, liebes Herz,
still und kühl verglühen
wird der heisse Schmerz.
Was den Winter über
oft enheilbar schien,
es entweicht das Fieber,
wenn die Rosen blüh'n.

When the roses bloom,
hope, dear heart,
the burning pain will cease,
will become still and cool.
Whatever during the winter
oft seemed incurable,
it escapes [will escape] the fever,
when the roses bloom.

Wenn die Rosen blühen,
matt gequältes Herz,
freue dich! wir ziehen
dann wohl himmelwärts.
Ewig dann genesen,
wirst du neu erglüh'n,
wirst ein himmlisch Wesen,
wenn die Rosen blüh'n.

When the roses bloom,
feeble, tormented heart,
rejoice! then, indeed,
we move toward heaven.
Then, forever recovered,
you will have new radiance,
you will become a heavenly being,
when the roses bloom.

179. IL BARBIERE DI SIVIGLIA, Act I, Recitative and Aria:
"La calunnia è un venticello"
Gioachino Rossini (1792–1868)

Il Barbiere Di Siviglia (The Barber of Seville), Act I, Recitative and Aria: "La calunnia è un venticello" Libretto by Cesare Sterbini Music by Gioacchino Rossini English Version—by Ruth and Thomas Martin Copyright © 1962 G. Schirmer, Inc. All Rights Reserved. Reprinted by Permission.

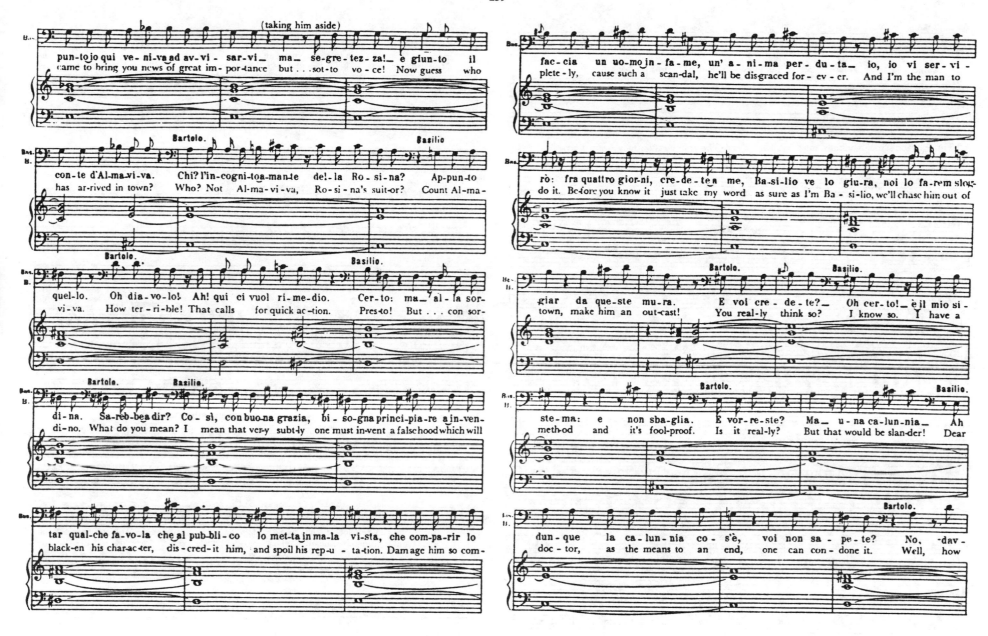

260

* The following aria is usually sung one tone lower. The transposition may begin here.

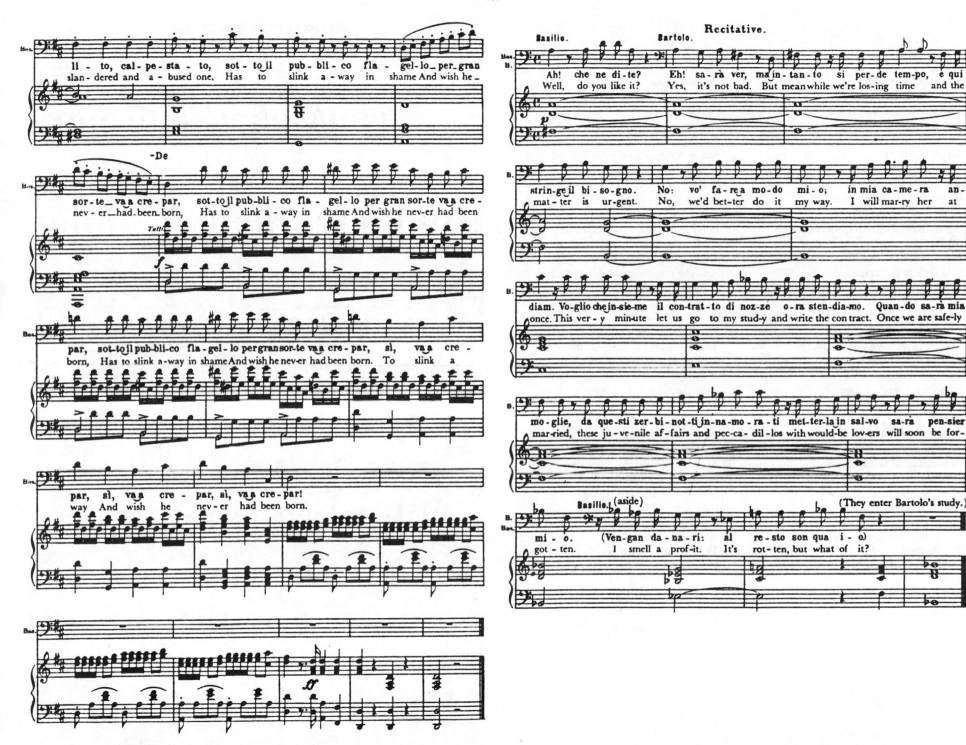

ARIA:

BASILIO:

La calunnia è un venticello,
Un' auretta assai gentille,
Che insensibile, sottile,
Leggermente, dolcemente,
Incomincia, incomincia susurar.

Piano, piano, terra, terra,
Sotto voce, sibilando,
Va scorrendo, va ronzando,
Va scorrendo, va ronzando,
Nelle orecchie della gente
S'introduce, s'introduce destramente,

E le teste, ed i cervelli,
E le teste, ed i cervelli,
Fa stordire, fa stordire, e fa gonfiar.

Della bocca fuori ascendo,
La schiamazzo va crescendo,
Prende forza poco a poco,
Vola già di loco in loco
Sembra il tuono la tempesta,
Che nel sen della foresta
Va fischiando, brontolando,
E ti fa d'orror gelar;
Alla fin trabocca e scoppia,
Si propaga, si raddoppia,
E produce un' esplosione
Come un colpo di cannone,
Come un colpo di cannone,
Un tremoto, un temporale,
Un tremoto generale,
Che fa l'aria rimbombar,
Si, che fa l'aria rimbombar.

E il meschino calcunniato,
Avvilito, calpestato,
Sotto il publico flagello,

Per gran sorte va a crepar.

—Cesare Sterbini

BASILIO:

Slander is a whisper,
A little breeze quite gentle,
That imperceptible, subtle,
Lightly, quietly,
Commences, begins to murmur.

Softly, softly, close to the ground,
In a low voice, hissing,
It flows along, it goes humming,
It goes flying, it goes buzzing,
In the ears of the people
It is introduced, it is slipped in
    dextrously
And the witness, and the brains,
And the testimony, and the sense,
Is made dizzy, is stunned, and is filled
    with air.

Rising from the mouth,
The cackling [or, clamor] increases,
Getting stronger little by little,
It flies, of course, from place to place,
Like the roar of a tempest
That in the bosom of the forest
Goes whistling, rumbling,
And makes you have chills of terror;
Finally, it brims over and it bursts,
So it spreads, so it redoubles,
And creates an explosion
Like a shot from a cannon,
Like a shot from a cannon,
A whirlwind, a thunderstorm,
A general earthquake,
That makes the air reverberate,
Yes, that makes the air re-echo.

And the wretched person slandered,
Humiliated, downtrodden,
Under public beating [= tongue-
    lashing],
Through [this] great destiny is ruined.

180. PRELUDE, Op. 28, No. 4
Frédéric Chopin (1810–1849)

Source: European American Music Distributors, PA

181. ÉTUDE, Op. 25, No. 11, "Winter Wind"
Frédéric Chopin (1810–1849)

Source: European American Music Distributors, PA

182. NOCTURNE, Op. 32, No. 2
Frédéric Chopin (1810–1849)

Source: Polskie Wydawnictwo Muzyczne, New York, N.Y.

183. CONCERTO in E Minor, for Violin and Orchestra, mvt. 1
Felix Mendelssohn (1809-1847)

Source: Breitkopf & Härtel, Wiesbaden

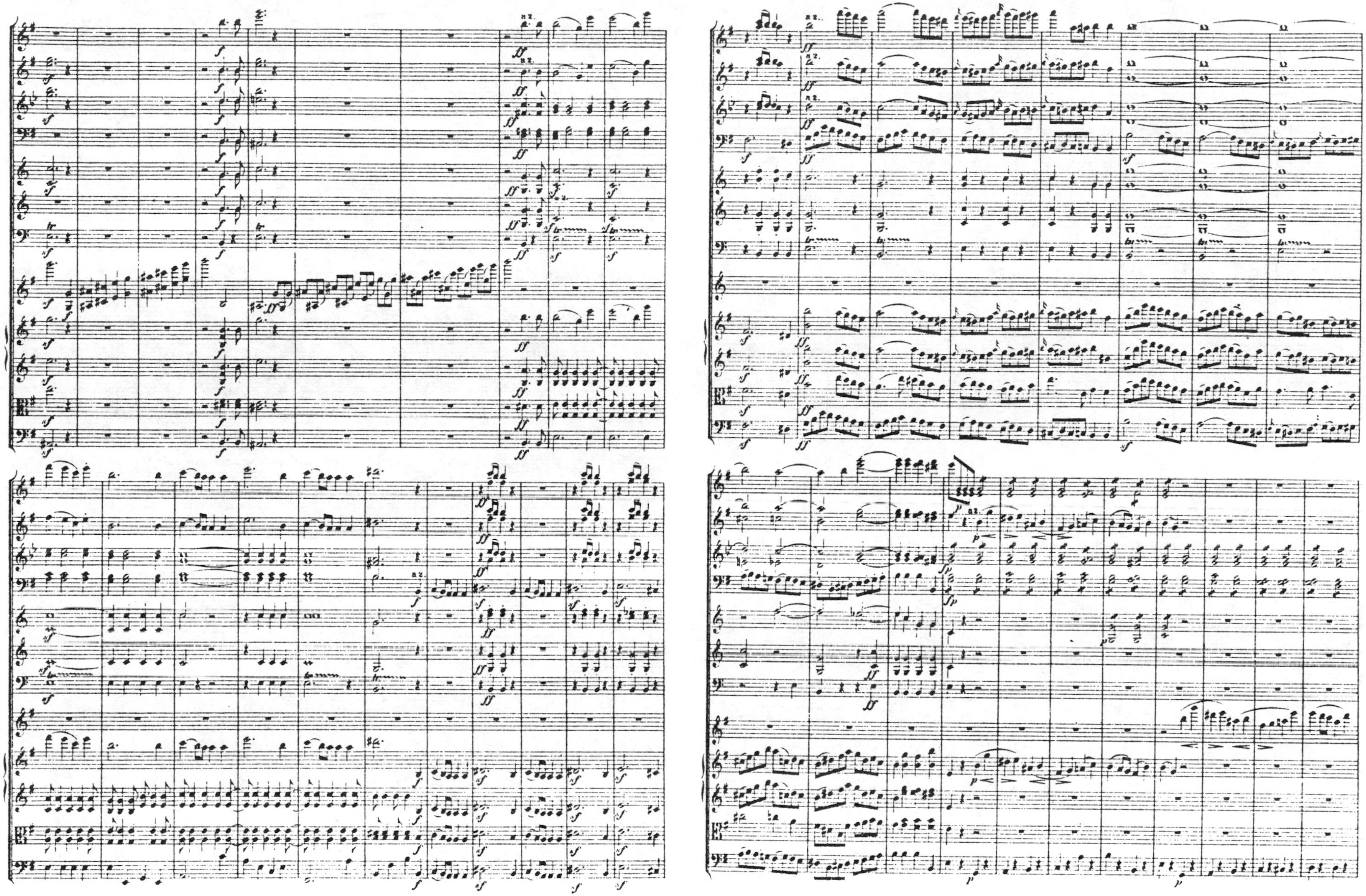
a 2.

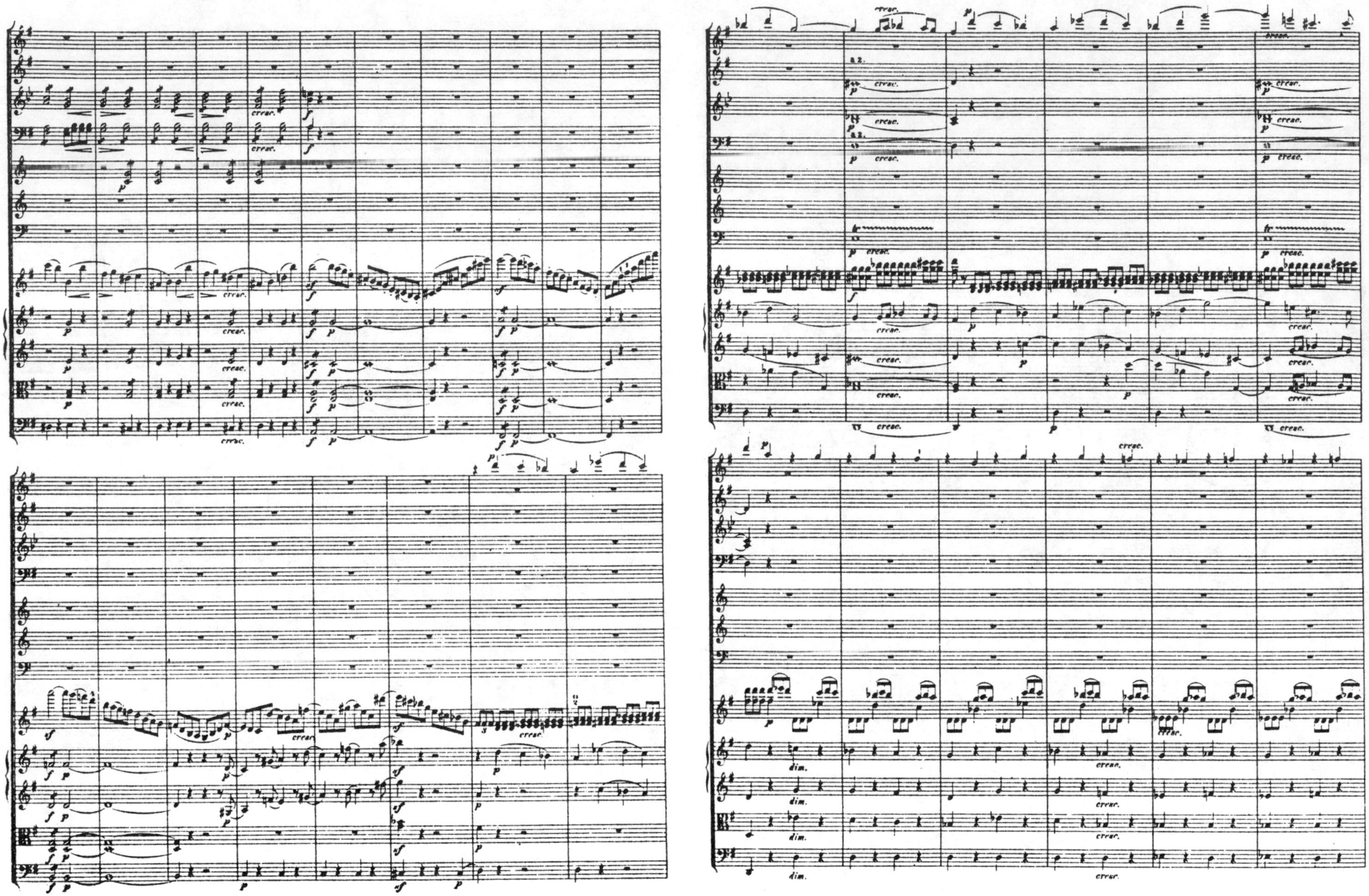
cresc.
a 2.
dim.

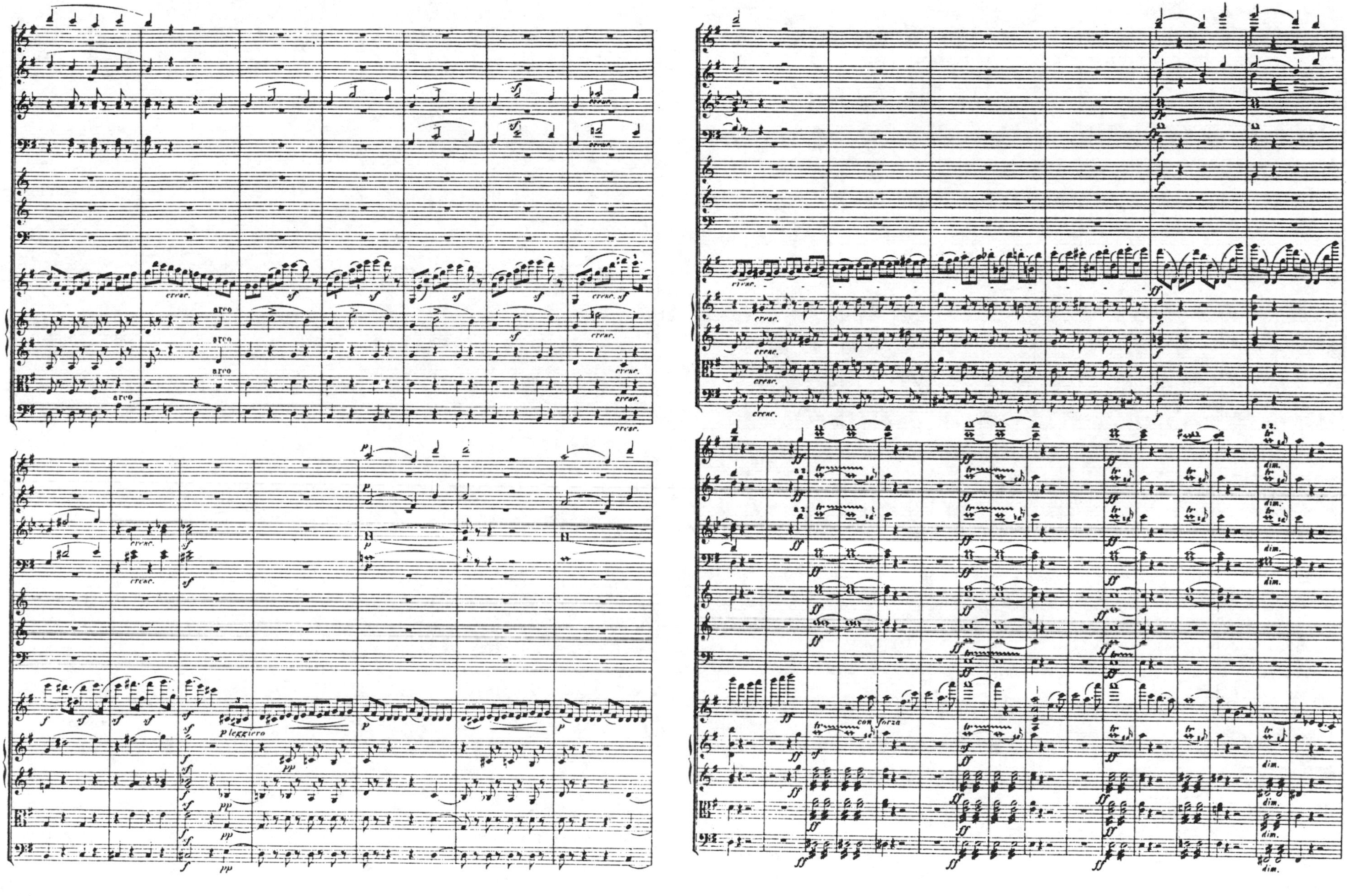

cresc.
arco
p leggiero
con forza
a 2.
dim.

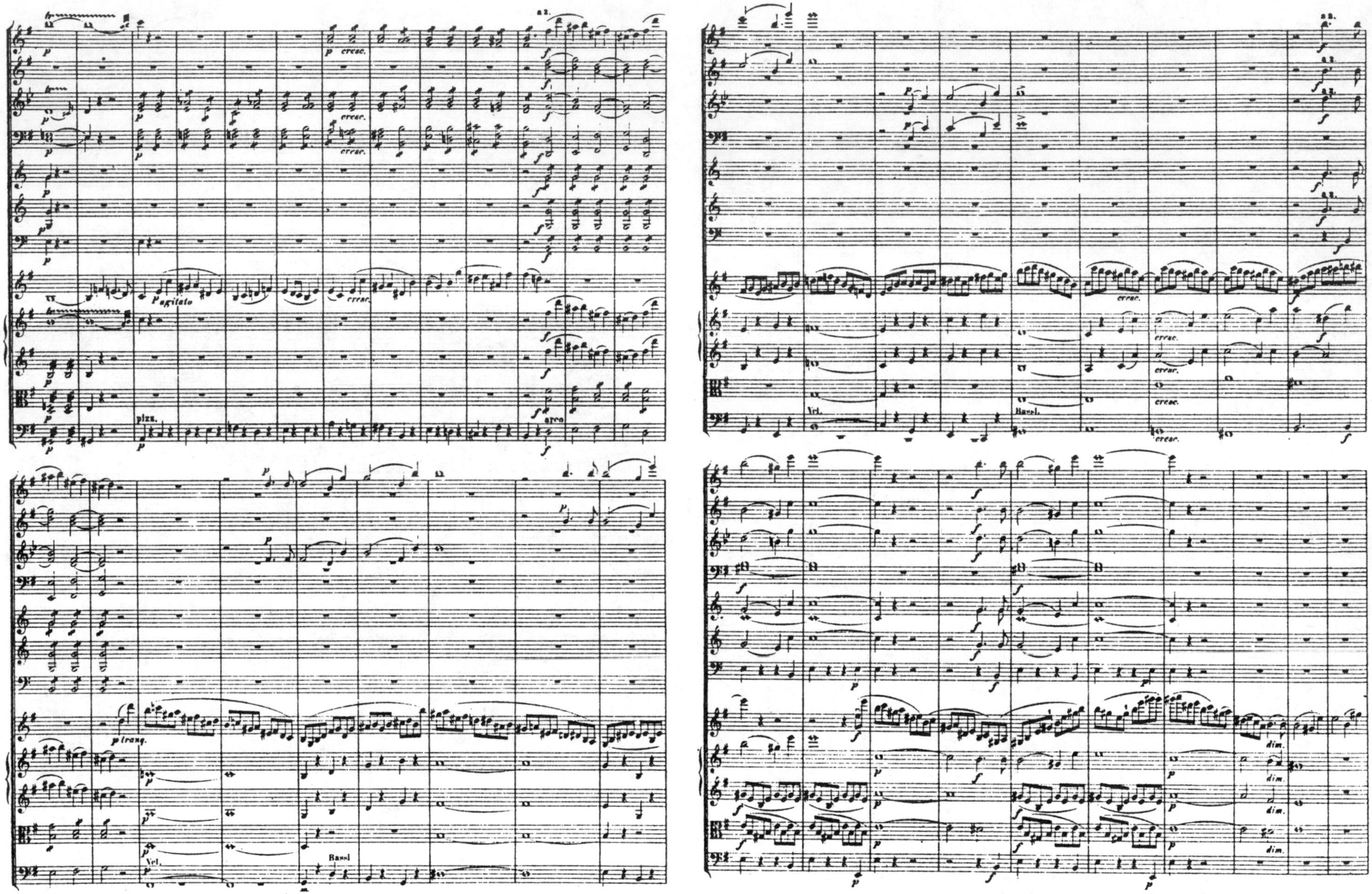
a 2.
p
cresc.
f
agitato
pizz.
arco
Vcl.
Bassi
Bassi
p tranq.
dim.

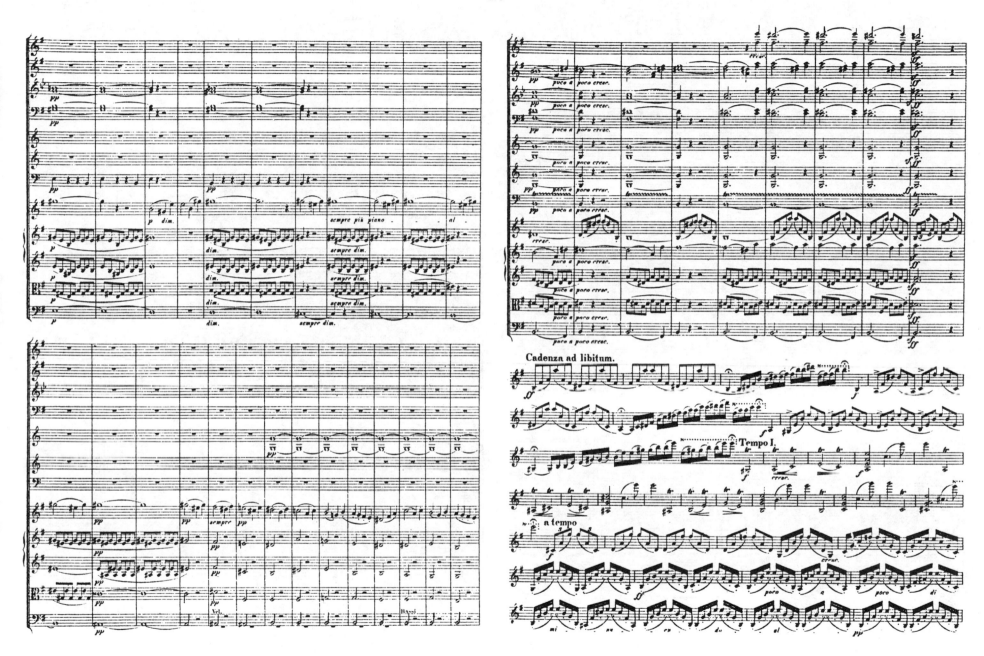

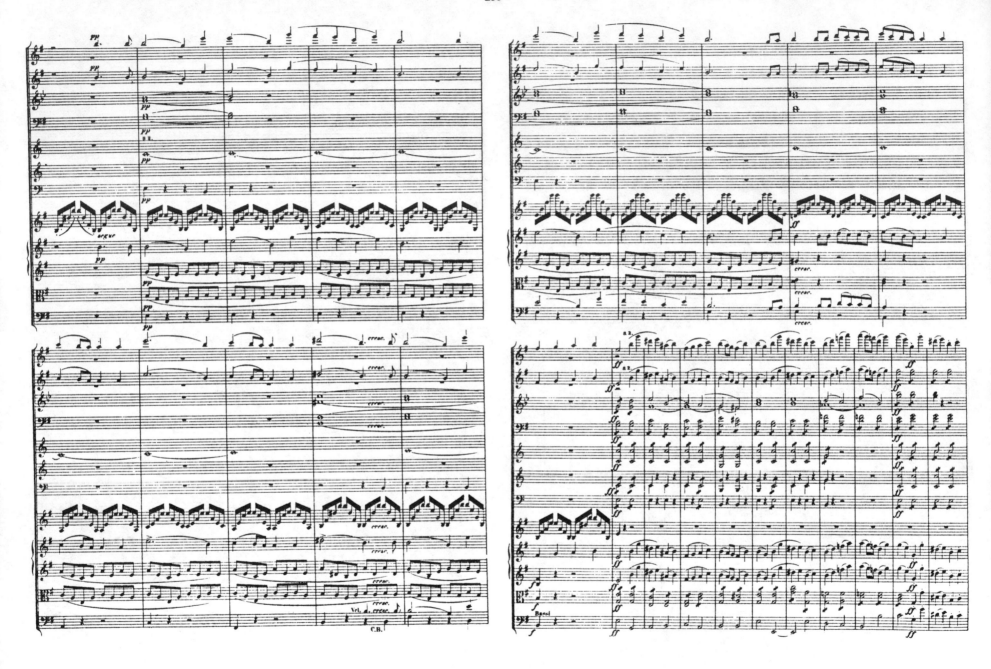

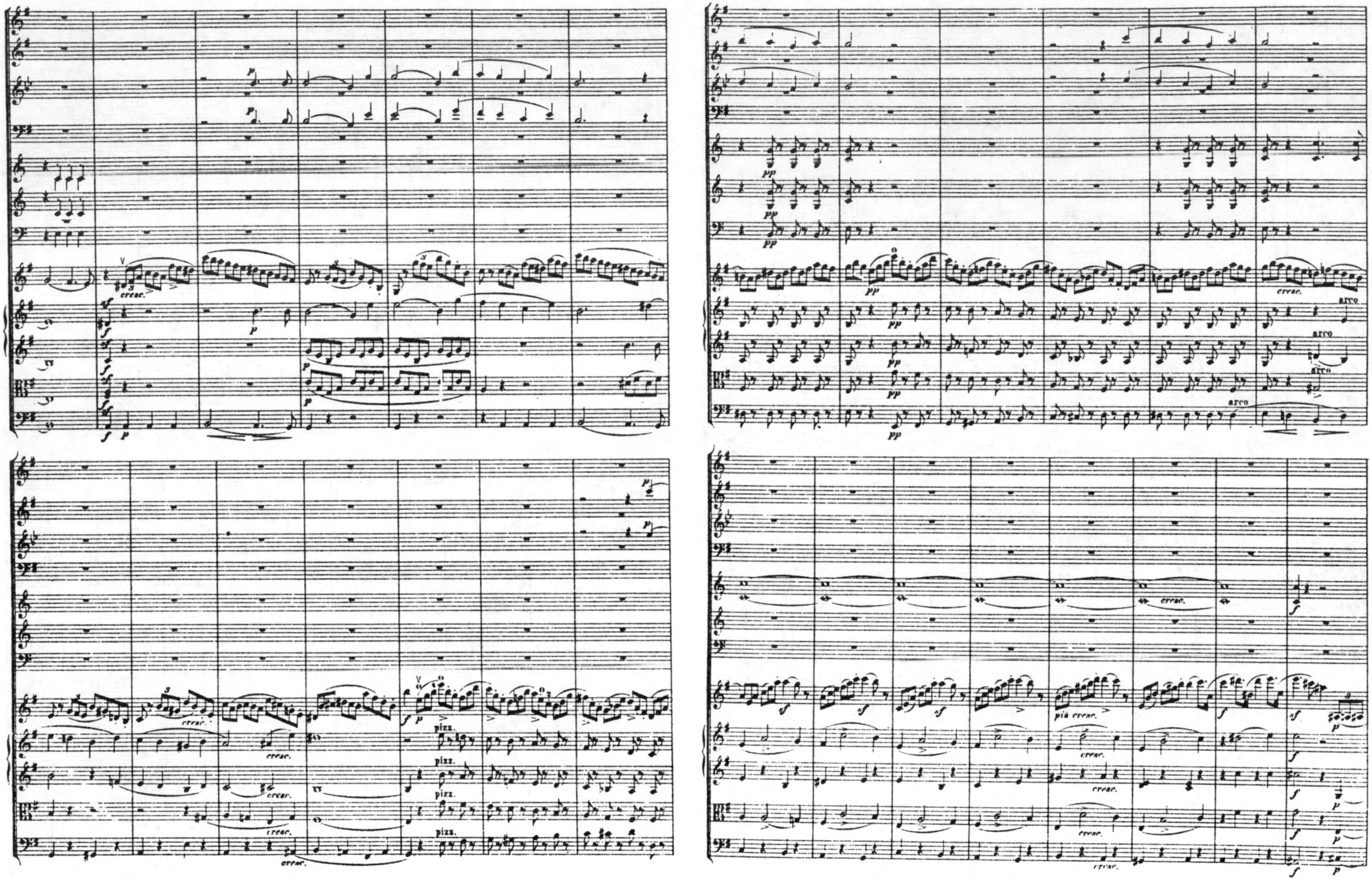
cresc.
pizz.
arco
più cresc.

Più presto.

Sempre più presto.

Presto.

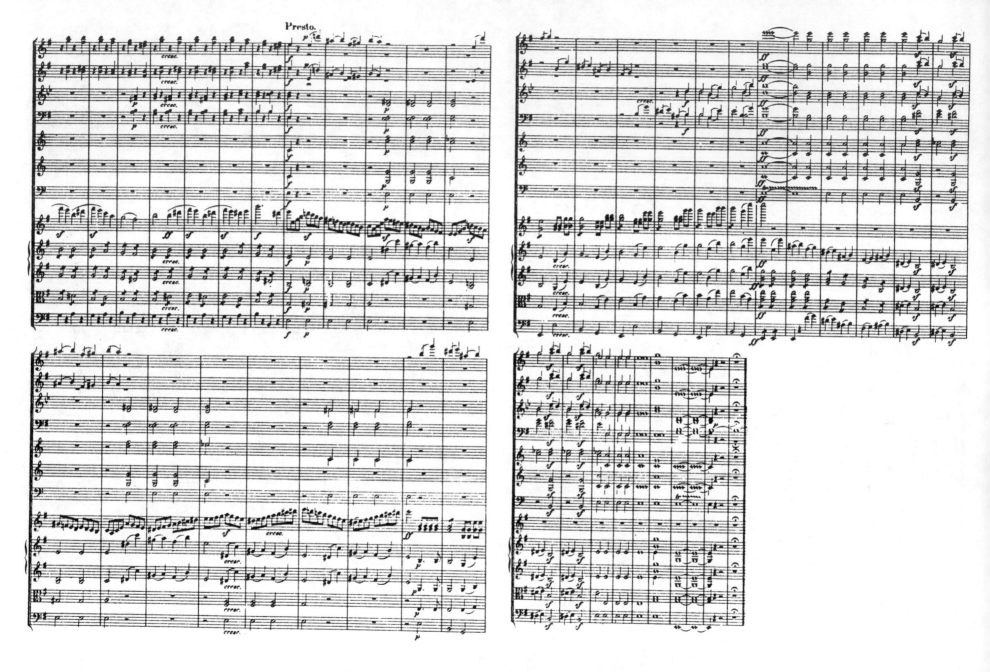

184. ELIAS, Oratorio, Nos. 10-16
Felix Mendelssohn (1809-1847)

ELIJAH. Op. 70. Felix Mendelssohn. Kalmus Miniature Scores #500. Belwin-Mills Publishing Corp. c/o CPP/Belwin Inc., Miami, FL 33014 Reprinted by consent of the publisher

No. 15 was omitted from record set.

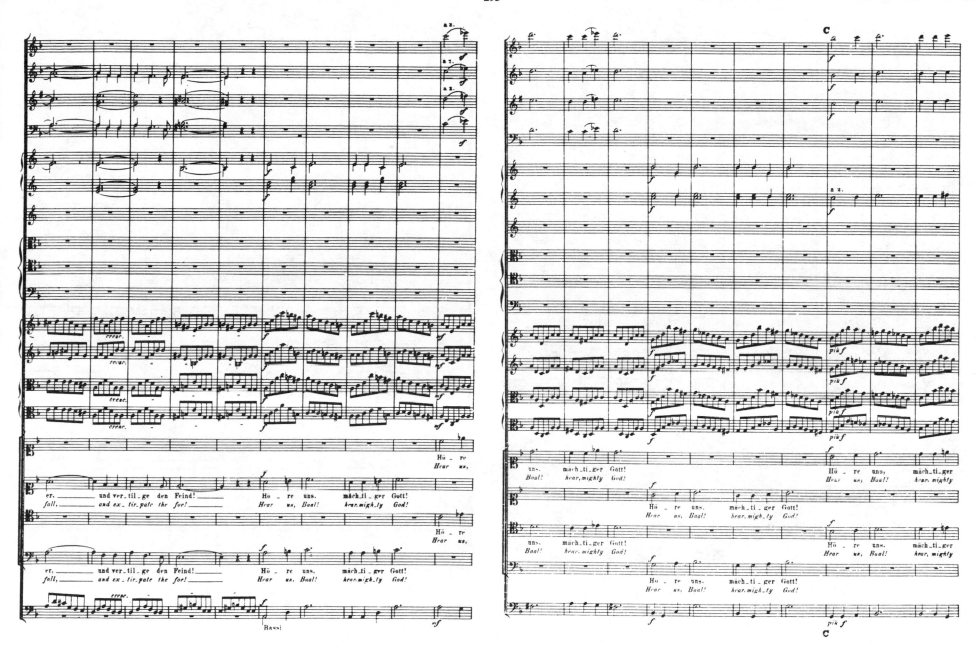

Nº 12. RECITATIVO e CORO.

Adagio. ♩=63

in B.

in Es.

Baal! Baal! gib uns Antwort, gib uns Antwort, gib uns Antwort, gib uns Antwort!

Baal! Baal! hear and answer, hear and answer, hear and answer! hear and answer!

Baal! Baal! gib uns Antwort, gib uns Antwort, gib uns Antwort. gib uns Antwort!

Baal! Baal! hear and answer, hear and answer, hear and answer! hear and answer!

Elias.
Kommt her, al les Volk, kommt her zu mir!
Draw near all ye peo ple, come to me!

Adagio.

Bassi

Nº16. RECITATIVO con CORO.

185. DER NUSSBAUM, Op. 25, No. 3, Lied
Robert Schumann (1810–1856)

Source: Breitkopf & Härtel, Wiesbaden

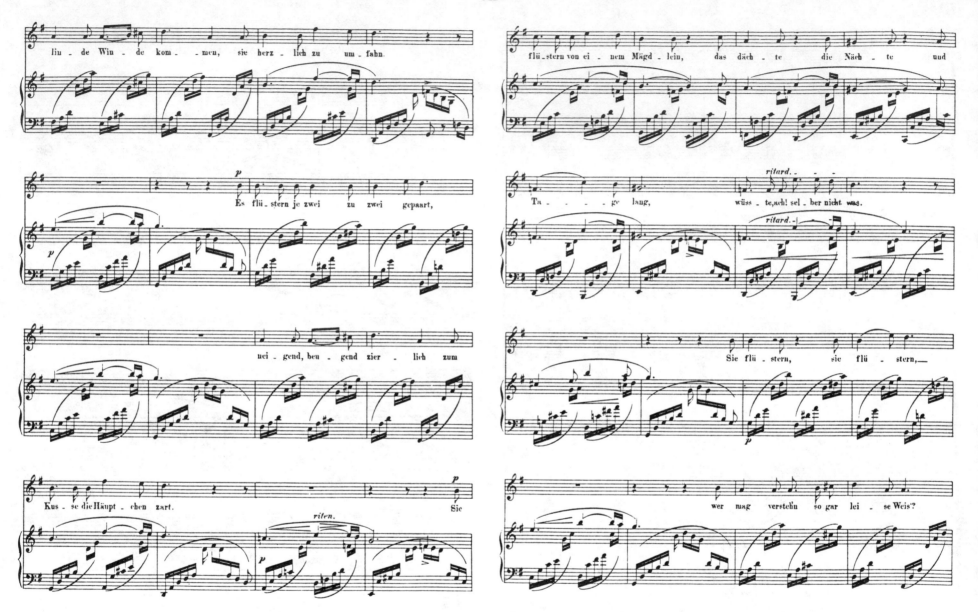

Es grünet ein Nussbaum vor dem Haus,

duftig, luftig, breitet er blättrig die Äste aus.
Viel liebliche Blüthen stehen d'ran;
linde Winde kommen; sie herzlich zu umfah'n.
Es flüstern je zwei zu zwei gepaart,
neigend, beugend zierlich zum kusse die Häuptchen zart.
Sie flüstern von einem Mägdlein,
das dächte die Nächte und Tage lang,
wusste, ach! selber nicht, was.
Sie flüstern, wer mag versteh'n so gar leise Weis?
flüstern vom Bräut'gam und nächstem Jahr.
Das Mägdlein horchet, es rauscht im Baum;
sehnend, wähnend, sinkt es
lächelnd in Schlaf und Traum.

—J. Mosen

There is a nut tree greening in front of the house,
fragrant, airy, it spreads out the leafy boughs.
Many lovely buds stand thereon;
gentle breezes come to embrace them affectionately.
Paired, they whisper, two by two,
bending, bowing down gracefully to kiss the delicate little heads.
They whisper of a young maiden,
who thought the nights and days long,
alas! she knew not what.
They whisper, who can understand such very soft music?
[they] whisper of bridegroom and next year.
The young maiden listens, it rustles in the tree;
longing, hoping, she sinks
smiling into sleep and dream.

186. CARNAVAL, Op. 9, Excerpts
Robert Schumann (1810–1856)

a. Eusebius

b. Florestan

Source: Breitkopf & Hartel, Wiesbaden

c. Sphinxes

d. Chiarina

e. Chopin

g. **Paganini**

f. Estrella

317

187. DIE BEIDEN GRENADIERE, Op. 49, No. 1, Ballad
Robert Schumann (1810–1856)

Source: Breitkopf & Härtel, Wiesbaden

319

Nach Frankreich zogen zwei Grenadier'

die waren in Russland gefangen.
Und als sie kamen ins deutsche
    Quartier,
sie liessen die köpfe hangen.

Da hörten sie Beide die traurige Mähr!
dass Frankreich verloren gegangen,
besiegt und geschlagen das tapfere Heer,
und der Kaiser gefangen!

Da weinten zusammen die Grenadier',
wohl ob der kläglichen Kunde.
Der Eine sprach: "Wie weh wird mir,
wie brennt meine alte Wunde!"

Der Andre sprach: "Das Lied ist aus,
auch ich möcht' mit dir sterben,
doch hab' ich Weib und Kind zu Haus,
die ohne mich verderben."

"Was schert mich Weib, was schert
    mich Kind,
ich trage weit bess'res Verlangen;
lass sie betteln geh'n, wenn sie hungrig
    sind,—
mein Kaiser, mein Kaiser, gefangen!

To France were returning two
    grenadiers
who had been captured in Russia.
And when they came into the German
    quarter,
they hung their heads.

There they both heard the sad news!
that France was lost,
the brave army defeated and conquered
and the emperor captured!

There the grenadiers wept together
about the deplorable news.
One spoke: "Woe is me,
how my old wound burns!"

The other spoke: "The song has ended,*
also, I would like to die with you,
but I have a wife and child at home,
who would perish without me."

"What care I for wife, what care I for
    child,
I have far better desires;
let them go begging when they are
    hungry,—
my emperor, my emperor, captured!

"Gewähr' mir, Bruder, eine Bitt':
Wenn ich jetzt sterben werde,
so nimm meine Leiche nach Frankreich
    mit,
begrab' mich in Frankreichs Erde.

"Das Ehrenkreuz am rothen Band
sollst du auf's Herz mir legen;
die Flinte gieb mir in die Hand,
und gürt' mir um den Degen.

"So will ich liegen und horchen still,
wie eine Schildwach' im Grabe,
bis einst ich höre Kanonengebrüll
und wiehernder Rosse Getrabe.

"Dann reitet mein Kaiser wohl über
    mein Grab,
viel' Schwerter klirren und blitzen;
dann steig' ich gewaffnet hervor aus
    dem Grab,
den Kaiser, den Kaiser zu schützen!"

—Heinrich Heine

"Grant me, brother, one request:
When I die now,
then take my corpse to France with you,

bury me in French soil.

"The cross of honor on the red ribbon
you shall lay on my heart;
put my musket in my hand,
and gird my sword around me.

"So will I lie and listen quietly,
like a sentry in the grave,
till one day I hear the roar of cannons
and neighing horses' trotting.

"Then surely my emperor rides over
    my grave,
many swords clash and flash;
then I will rise, armed, from the grave,

the emperor, the emperor to defend!"

*It's all over.

188. MONDNACHT, Op. 39, No. 5, Lied
Robert Schumann (1810–1856)

Source: Breitkopf & Härtel, Wiesbaden

Es war, als hätt' der Himmel
die Erde still geküsst,
dass sie im Blüthenschimmer

von ihm nur träumen müsst'.

Die Luft ging durch die Felder,
die Ähren wogten sacht,
es rauschten leis' die Wälder,
so sternklar war die Nacht.

Und meine Seele spannte
weit ihre Flügel aus,
flog durch die stillen Lande,
als flöge sie nach Haus.

—Eichendorff

It was as if heaven had
quietly kissed the earth,
that in the flowers' splendor it [i.e., earth]
must dream only of him [i.e., heaven].

The breeze went through the fields,
the [wheat]heads billowed gently,
it softly rustled the woodlands,
so starlit was the night.

And my soul spread
wide its wings,
flew over the silent lands,
as though flying home.

189. LIEBST DU UM SCHÖNHEIT, Lied,
Clara Schumann (1819-1896)

Source: Breitkopf & Härtel, Wiesbaden

Liebst du um Schönheit, o nicht mich liebe!

Liebe die Sonne, sie trägt ein goldnes Haar!

Liebst du um Jugend, o nicht mich liebe!

Liebe den Frühling, der jung ist jedes Jahr!

Liebst du um Schätze, o nicht mich liebe!

Liebe die Meerfrau, sie hat viel Perlen klar!

Liebst du um Liebe, o ja, mich liebe!

Liebe mich immer, dich lieb' ich immer, immerdar!

—Friedrich Rückert

If you love for beauty, oh, do not love me!

Love the sun, it wears golden hair!

If you love for youth, oh, do not love me!

Love the spring, which is young every year!

If you love for treasures, oh, do not love me!

Love the mermaid, she has many bright pearls!

If you love for love, oh yes, love me!

Love me always, [for] I love you always, forevermore!

190. LES HUGUENOTS, Act IV, Scenes 22, 23
Giacomo Meyerbeer (1791–1864)

Entr'acte, Recitative, Romanza, and Scene, proceeding directly into Conjuration and Benediction of Daggers

Source: Reprinted from Les Huguenots (Paris: Ph. MAQUET & Cie., not dated.)

ROMANZA

324

326

CONJURATION

329

NEVERS (avec indignation)

V. Que va-t-il di _ re? Je tremble,hélas! *f* Frappous nos en_ne_mis,mais non pas sans dé_

St BRIS

N. _fen_se; Ce n'est pas le poignard qui doit percer leur sein! Quand le roi le comman_de!..

NEVERS (avec dignité)

Il me commande en vain De flé_trir de mon sang l'honneur et la bra_

(avec force)

N. _vou _ re....... Et par_mi ces il_lus_tres a_ïeux dont la gloi_re ici même_

_tou _ re, Je comp_te des sol_dats, je compte des sol_dats et pas un as_sas_

St BRIS   NEVERS

N. _sin! Quoi! par toi notre cause est trahie et trompé_e! Non! mais du déshonneur je sauve mon é_

(Il brise son épée)

N. _pé _ e! Tiens! tiens! la voi _ là! Que Dieu

BÉNÉDICTION DES POIGNARDS

(sans le 1er Moine)

cel _ _ le Pour servir le Sei _ gneur!

(Tous les assistants tirent leurs épées et leurs poignards; les moines bénissent les armes

St. BRIS et les 3 Moines (étendant les mains)

Glai _ ves pi _ eux _ saintes é _ pé _ es, Qui dans un

sang impur serez bien _ tôt trempé _ es, Vous par qui le Très-Haut frappe ses ennemis,

Glai _ ves _ pi _ eux, par nous soy_ez _ bé _ nis! Oui, gloire au Dieu ven_geur,

Glai _ ves _ pi _ eux, par nous soy_ez _ bé _ nis! Oui, gloire au Dieu ven_geur,

Sop.

Tén.

Gloi _

Basses

Gloi _

Gloi _

1er MOINE

Oui, gloire au Dieu ven_geur,

344

348

The setting is an apartment in the hotel of Count de Nevers. There are two doors: one leads into Valentine's bedroom; the other, hidden by a tapestry, leads into a study. A window looks out on the street.

VALENTINE
Je suis seul chez moi, seul avec ma
  doulour!
À d'éternels tourments vous m'avez
  condamnée, Mon père!
Un autre avait mon coeur,
Et pourtant vous m'avez donnée!

VALENTINE
I am alone in my home, alone with my
  grief!
You have condemned me to eternal
  torments, my father!
Another had my heart,
And yet you have given me [in
  marriage]!

Et vous que j'implorais en vain dans
  mon malheur,
Vous qui l'avez permis, ce funeste
  hyménée,
Mon Dieu, daignez du moins, pour
  alleger mes maux,
Chasser un souvenir fatal à mon repos!

And You whom I implored in vain in my
  distress,
You who have allowed it, this fatal
  marriage,
My God, deign at least, to alleviate my
  sufferings,
to drive away a memory fatal to my
  peace!

(Valentine sings this ROMANZA)

Parmi les pleurs mon rêve se ranime;
C'est à lui seul qu'appartiennent mes
  jours—mes jours.
Ces doux regrets, y penser est un crime;

je veux les fuir, je veux les fuir,—hélas!
et j'y pense toujours—toujours!

Amid the tears, my dream revives;
It is to him alone that my days belong—
  my days.
These sweet regrets, to think of them is
  a crime;
I want to flee from them, (repeated)
  alas! and I think of them always—
  always!

De loin encor sa voix chérie, oui,
  même ici sa voix chérie
Fait taire en moi la voix des cieux;
Et son image, quand je prie,
Sur les autels, hélas! s'offre, s'offre
  à mes yeux—(repeated)
s'offre à mes yeux!
Raoul, cher Raoul!
quelle est donc sa puissance?
De Dieu lui-même il est vainqueur!
Ah! que me sert d'éviter sa presence?

From far away his dear voice, yes,
  even here his dear voice
silences in me the voice of the heavens;
And his image, when I pray,
on the altars, alas! offers itself,
  offers itself to my eyes—(repeated)
  offers itself to my eyes!
Raoul, dear Raoul!
what, then, is his power?
He is the conqueror of God himself!
Ah! what good does it do me to avoid his
  presence?

Je le retrouve toujours dans mon coeur!
Ah! que me sert . . . (repeated)

I find him again always in my heart!
Ah! what good does it do me . . .
  (repeated)

Hélas! hélas!
Mon Dieu! je le retrouve toujours, hélas!

Alas! alas!
My God! I find him again always, alas!

(Raoul appears in the doorway.)

VALENTINE continues:
Juste ciel! est-ce lui?
  lui dont l'aspect terrible
Ainsi que le remords sans cesse me
  poursuit?

VALENTINE continues:
Just heaven! Is it he?
  he, whose terrible appearance,
as well as remorse, pursues me
  incessantly?

RAOUL
Oui, c'est moi! moi, qui
    viens dans l'ombre et dans la nuit,
Ainsi qu'un criminel, dont la peine est
    horrible,
Et qui, las de souffrir, succombe au
    despoir!

VALENTINE
Que voulez-vous de moi?

RAOUL
Rien! j'ai voulu vous voir avant que de
    mourir!

VALENTINE
Qu'entends-je? est-il possible?
Est mon père! et mon mari!

RAOUL
Oui, je pouvais les rencontrer ici;
Je le savais!

VALENTINE
Leur coeur est inflexible;
Ils vous tueraient! Fuyez!

RAOUL
Non, j'attendrai leurs coups!

VALENTINE
Entendez-vous ces pas? Fuyez!

RAOUL
Non, non, je reste . . .
Et si quelque danger . . .

VALENTINE
Mon père! mon époux!
Pour moi . . . pour mon honneur,
    évitez leur courroux!

(She hides Raoul behind the tapestry, in the room at the side.)

RAOUL
Yes, it is I, who
    come in the shadow and in the night,
Just as a criminal, whose suffering is
    horrible,
And who, weary of suffering, succumbs
    to despair!

VALENTINE
What do you want from me?

RAOUL
Nothing! I wanted to see you before I
    die!

VALENTINE
What do I hear? Is it possible?
It is my father! and my husband!

RAOUL
Yes, I might encounter them here;
I knew it!

VALENTINE
Their hearts are inflexible;
They would kill you! Flee!

RAOUL
No, I will await their blows!

VALENTINE
Do you hear those footsteps? Flee!

RAOUL
No, no, I am staying . . .
And if some danger . . .

VALENTINE
My father! my husband!
For me . . . for my honor,
    avoid their wrath!

SCENE: St. Bris, Nevers, Tavannes, and some other Catholic nobles enter.

ST. BRIS
Oui, l'ordre de la reine en ces lieux vous
    rassemble.
L'heure est enfin venue où je dois à vos
    yeux
Devoiler des projets protégés par les
    cieux,
Et dès longtemps conçus par Medicis.

VALENTINE
Je tremble!

ST. BRIS (to Valentine)
Vous, ma fille, sortez!

VALENTINE
Mon père!

NEVERS
Pourquoi donc?
Son zèle ardent pour la foi catholique
Permet que sans danger devant elle on
    explique
De la reine et du ciel les ordres absolus.

ST. BRIS
Yes, the queen's order musters you in
    this locality.
Finally, the hour has come when I must
    reveal to your eyes
some projects protected by heaven,

and conceived a long time ago by
    Medicis.

VALENTINE
I tremble!

ST. BRIS
You, my daughter, leave!

VALENTINE
My father!

NEVERS
But why?
Her ardent zeal for the Catholic faith
allows us, without danger, to explain
    before her
the absolute orders of the queen and of
    heaven.

CONJURATION

SAINT-BRIS (to the Nobles)
Des troubles renaissants et d'une guerre
    impie
Voulez-vous, comme moi, délivrez le
    pays?

4 NOBLES
C'est notre voeu, c'est notre voeu!

SAINT-BRIS
Du trône et du ciel, du ciel, de la patrie,
Voulez-vous, comme moi, frapper les
    ennemis?

SAINT-BRIS
Do you wish, as I do, to deliver the
    country from recurring troubles and
    an impious war?

4 NOBLES
It is our wish!

SAINT-BRIS
Are you willing, as I am, to strike the
    enemies of the throne, of heaven, and
    of the country?

NOBLES
Nous sommes prêts, nous sommes prêts!

SAINT-BRIS
Eh, bien! Du Dieu qui nous protège
Le glaive menaçant est sur eux sus
  pendu;
Des huguenots la race sacrilège
Aura dès aujourd'hui pour jamais
  disparu!

NEVERS
Mais . . . qui les condamne?

SAINT-BRIS
Dieu!

4 NOBLES
Dieu!

NEVERS
Et qui les frappera?

SAINT-BRIS
Nous!

NOBLES
Nous!

NEVERS
Nous? Nous?

SAINT-BRIS
Pour cette cause sainte
J'obéirai sans crainte,
J'obéirai sans crainte
À mon Dieu, à mon Dieu, à mon roi.
Comptez sur mon courage;
Entre vos mains j'engage,
Entre vos mains j'engage
Mes serments, mes serments et ma foi,
  mes serments et ma foi.

échos of
le Marseillaise

NOBLES
We are ready!

SAINT-BRIS
Well! For God, who protects us,
the menacing sword is suspended over
  them;
The sacrilegious race of Huguenots
from this day will have disappeared
  forever!

NEVERS
But . . . who condemns them?

SAINT-BRIS
God!

NOBLES
God!

NEVERS
And who will strike them?

SAINT-BRIS
We!

NOBLES
We!

NEVERS
We? We will?

SAINT-BRIS
For this holy cause
I will obey without fear,
I will obey without fear
for my God, for my God, for my king.
Count on my courage;
Into your hands I place,
In your hands I place
my oaths, my vows and my faith, my
  vows and my faith.

Together

NEVERS
Quel est donc ce langage?
À l'honneur seul j'engage
mes serments et ma foi!

TAVANNES, SAINT-BRIS
Comptez sur mon courage!
Entre vos mains j'engage
Mes serments, et ma foi,
A mon Dieu, à mon roi.

NOBLES
Grand Dieu, sauvez, sauvez la foi!
Dieu, sauvez, Dieu, sauvez notre foi,
  sauvez la foi!
J'obéis à mon roi! à mon roi!

VALENTINE
Comment tromper leur rage?
Dieu, soutiens mon courage,
Et prends pitié de moi, pitié, pitié de
  moi!
Ah, grand Dieu, prends pitié! (repeat
  the line)

SAINT-BRIS
Le roi peut-il compter sur vous?

NOBLES
Nous le jourons!

SAINT-BRIS
C'est moi qui dois guider vos pas!

NOBLES
Nous vous suivrons!

ALL BUT NEVERS
Quoi! Nevers seul a gardé le silence!

Together

NEVERS
What language is this?
To honor alone I pledge
my vows and my faith!

TAVANNES, SAINT-BRIS
Count on my courage!
Into your hands I place
my vows, and my faith,
For my God, for my king.

NOBLES
Almighty God, save, save the faith!
God, save, God, save our faith, save our
  faith!
I obey my king! for my king!

VALENTINE
How can I cheat their rage?
God, uphold my courage,
and have pity on me, pity, pity on me!

Ah, almighty God, have pity! (repeat
  the line)

SAINT-BRIS
Can the king count on you?

NOBLES
We swear it!

SAINT-BRIS
It is I who must guide your steps!

NOBLES
We will follow you!

ALL BUT NEVERS
What! Only Nevers kept silent!

ENSEMBLE: Nevers, St.-B., Tavannes, Nobles, and Valentine

356

VALENTINE
Que va-t-il dire? Je tremble, hélas!

NEVERS
Frappons nos ennemis, mais non pas sans défense.
Ce n'est pas le poignard qui doit percer leur sein!

SAINT-BRIS
Quand le roi le commande!

NEVERS
Il me commande en vain
De flétrir de mon sang l'honneur et la bravoure,
Et parmi ces illustres aïeux dont la gloire ici m'entoure,
Je compte des soldats, je compte des soldats et pas un assassin!

SAINT-BRIS
Quoi! par toi notre cause est trahie et trompée!

NEVERS
Non! mais du deshonneur je sauve mon épée!

(He breaks his sword.)

Tiens! tiens! la voilà!
Que Dieu juge entre nous!

VALENTINE (going to Nevers)
Ah! d' aujourd'hui tout mon sang est à vous, oui, d'aujourd'hui tout mon sang est à vous!
Vous saurez tout; venez, venez, venez, venez,
je dois vous apprendre . . .

(The main doors open, revealing officials, all armed.)

VALENTINE
What is he going to say? I tremble, alas!

NEVERS
Let us strike our enemies, but not without defense.
It is not the dagger that should pierce their breast!

SAINT-BRIS
Whenever the king commands it!

NEVERS
He commands me in vain
To stain with my blood honor and bravery,
And among the illustrious ancestors whose glory surrounds me,
I count some soldiers, I count some soldiers and not one assassin!

SAINT-BRIS
What! By you our cause is betrayed and cheated!

NEVERS
No! but I save my sword from dishonor!

See! Really! That's it!
Let God judge between us!

VALENTINE
Ah! from today all my blood is yours, yes, from today all my blood is yours!
You shall know everything; come, (repeated)
I must inform you . . .

SAINT-BRIS, to the people, and pointing to Nevers:
Assurez-vous de lui, de Nevers, de mon gendre;
Jusqu'à demain vous m'en répondez tous!

VALENTINE (aside)
Puisse le ciel désarmer son courroux!
Ah! . . .

NEVERS
Ma cause est juste et sainte!

SAINT-BRIS, TAVANNES, NOBLES
Pour cette cause sainte . . .

Together
NEVERS
Je puis, je dois sans crainte, . . .

VALENTINE
D'une mortelle crainte . . .

THE OTHERS
J'obéirai sans crainte, . . .

Together
NEVERS
je puis, je dois sans crainte, . . .

VALENTINE
Mon âme est atteinte!

Together
TAVANNES, SAINT-BRIS
. . . sans crainte à mon Dieu, à mon roi!

VALENTINE
Grand Dieu, prends pitié de moi!

NEVERS
. . . résister à moi roi!

THE OTHERS
. . . à notre roi, . . .

SAINT-BRIS
Take care of him, of Nevers, of my son-in-law;
Until tomorrow, all of you will answer to me!

VALENTINE
May heaven disarm his wrath!
Ah! . . .

NEVERS
My cause is just and sacred!

SAINT-BRIS, TAVANNES, NOBLES
For this sacred cause . . .

Together
NEVERS
I can, I must without fear. . .

VALENTINE
By a mortal fear . . .

THE OTHERS
I will obey without fear, . . .

Together
NEVERS
I can, I must without fear, . . .

VALENTINE
My soul is stricken!

Together
TAVANNES, SAINT-BRIS
. . . without fear, for my God, for my king!

VALENTINE
Great God, have pity on me!

NEVERS
. . . oppose my king!

THE OTHERS
. . . for our king, . . .

NEVERS
Je le puis, je le dois, . . .

Together

SAINT-BRIS
Recevez . . .

VALENTINE
Ah! grand Dieu, . . .

THE OTHERS
. . . à mon Dieu, . . .

SAINT-BRIS
. . . mes serments et ma foi,
et ma foi!

Together

VALENTINE
prends pitié! (repeated)

NEVERS
. . . résister à mon roi!

THE REST
. . . à mon roi! (repeated)

(Some men lead Nevers away; Valentine's father signals her to leave, and she exits.)

SAINT-BRIS
Et vous qui répondez au Dieu qui nous appelle,
chefs dévoués de la cité fidèle,
quarteniers, échevins, écoutez tous ma voix!
Qu'en ce riche quartier la foule répandue,
Sombre et silencieuse, occupe chaque rue,
Et qu'au même signal tous, tous, frappent à la fois!

CHORUS
Tous, tous, frappons à la fois!

NEVERS
I can [do] it, I must [do] it, . . .

Together

SAINT-BRIS
Receive . . .

VALENTINE
Oh! Almighty God, . . .

THE OTHERS
. . . for my God, . . .

SAINT-BRIS
. . . my vows and my faith,
and my faith!

Together

VALENTINE
have pity!

NEVERS
. . . oppose my king!

THE REST
. . . for my king!

SAINT-BRIS
And you who answer God, who calls you,
devoted heads of the faithful city,
mayors, magistrates, all listen to my voice!
Let the crowd circulate in this wealthy quarter,
somber and silent, occupy each street,

and, at the same signal, all, all, strike at the same time!

CHORUS
All, all, strike at the same time!

SAINT-BRIS
Toi, de Besme, et les tiens, entourez la demeure
De l'amiral; que le premier il meure!

CHORUS
Qu'il meure le premier!

SAINT-BRIS to another person
Vous, à l'hôtel de Nesle, où de nos ennemis
Tous les principaux chefs ce soir sont réunis
À la fête qu'on préparé
Pour Marguerite et le roi de Navarre.

CHORUS
Nous, à l'hôtel de Nesle!

SAINT-BRIS
Écoutez! écoutez! Lorsque de Saint Germain
Pour la première fois retentira l'airain,
Attentifs et muets à ce signal d'alarmes,
Dans l'ombre préparez vos soldats et vos armes.
Mais à ce lugubre appel, toi, cours partout éveiller le beffroi.
Je m'en remets à ta prudence!
Et lorsqu' enfin de l'Auxerrois
La cloche sainte aura pour la seconde fois
Du ciel impatient annoncé la vengeance,

Le fer en main, alors, levez-vous tous!
Que tout maudit expire sous vos coups!

Ce Dieu qui vous entend et vous béint d'avance,
Soldats chrétiens, marchera devant tous!

SAINT-BRIS
You, de Besme, and your people, surround the home
of the admiral; let him die first!

CHORUS
Let him die first!

SAINT-BRIS
You, to the hotel de Nesle, where all the

principal leaders of our enemies are assembled this evening
at the feast which they prepared
for Marguerite and the King of Navarre.

CHORUS
We, to the hotel de Nesle!

SAINT-BRIS
Listen! listen! When the bronze [bell] from
Saint Germain rings for the first time,
attentive and silent at this alarm signal,
in the dark prepare your soldiers and your arms.
But, at this lugubrious summons, you, run everywhere to sound the alarm.
I am relying on your prudence!
And when, finally, from Auxerrois
the sacred bell will have for the second time
announced the vengeance of impatient heaven,
then, sword in hand, all rise!
Let all the accursed die under your blows!
This God who hears you and blesses you in advance,
Christian soldiers, will march before you!

VALENTINE (looking out of her apartment)

Mon Dieu! Mon Dieu! comment le secourir?
Il doit entendre, hélas! et ne peut fuir!
Je veux, je veux et n'ose auprès de lui courir . . .
Dieu tout puissant! dans ce péril extrême
Sauvez Raoul, sauvez Raoul, et n'exposez que moi-même!

VALENTINE

My God! My God! how can I help him?
He must hear, alas! and he cannot flee!
I want, I want and I do not dare to run to his side . . .
Omnipotent God! in this extreme peril
save Raoul, save Raoul, and expose only me!

(Valentine withdraws.)

BENEDICTION OF DAGGERS
(3 monks enter from back of stage and advance slowly.)

MONKS and SAINT-BRIS

Gloire, gloire au grand Dieu vengeur!
Gloire au guerrier fidèle,
Dont le glaive étincelle
Pour servir le Seigneur, (repeat last 2 lines)!

MONKS and SAINT-BRIS

Glory, glory to the great avenger God!
Glory to the faithful warrior,
whose sword flashes
to serve the Lord, (repeat last 2 lines)!

(All present who have swords draw them, and the monks bless swords and daggers.)

Glaives pieux! saintes épées,
Qui dans un sang impur serez bientôt trempées,
Vous par qui le Très-Haut frappe ses ennemis,
Glaives pieux, par nous soyez bénis! Oui,
ALL
gloire au Dieu vengeur, (repeated)!

Pious swords! sacred rapiers,
that soon will be steeped in an impure blood,
you through whom the Most High strikes his enemies,
pious swords, be blessed by us! Yes,
ALL
glory to the avenger God, (repeated)!

(The first 4 lines sung by Saint-Bris and Monks are now sung by all.)

SAINT-BRIS

Que cette écharpe blanche et cette croix sans tache
Du ciel, du ciel distinguent les élus!

SAINT-BRIS

Let this white scarf and this unblemished cross
distinguish heaven's elect!

3 MONKS and SAINT-BRIS

Ni grâce, ni pitié!
Frappez tous sans relâche.
L'ennemi qui s'enfuit, l'ennemi qui se cache,

ALL OTHERS

Frappons, (repeat 5 times more)!

ST.-BRIS and MONKS

Le guerrier suppliant à vos pieds abattu!

ALL OTHERS

Frappons, (repeat 2 times more)!

SAINT-BRIS and MONKS

Ni grâce, ni pitié!
Que le fer et la flamme,
Atteignent le vieillard et l'enfant et la femme!
Anathème sur eux!

ALL ON STAGE

Anathème sur eux!

SAINT-BRIS and MONKS

Dieu ne les connaît pas!

ALL

Dieu le veut, Dieu l'ordonne!
Non! non! grâce à personne!
À ce prix il pardonne
Au pêcheur, au pêcheur répentant.
Que le glaive étincelle,
Que le sang ruiselle,
Et la palme immortelle
Dans le ciel vous attend!
(1st 4 lines are repeated)
Dieu le veut, Dieu l'ordonne,
N'épargnons personne!
(various lines are repeated)

SAINT-BRIS

Silence, mes amis!

MONKS and SAINT-BRIS

Neither mercy, nor pity!
Strike all without interruption.
The enemy who flees, the enemy who hides,

ALL OTHERS

Strike, (repeated)!

SAINT-BRIS and MONKS

The fallen warrior pleading at your feet!

ALL OTHERS

Strike, (repeated)!

SAINT-BRIS and MONKS

Neither mercy, nor pity!
Let the sword and the fire
reach old man, child, and woman!

A curse on them!

ALL ON STAGE

Anathema on them!

SAINT-BRIS and MONKS

God does not know them!

ALL

God wills it, God ordains it!
No! no! mercy for no one!
At this price he pardons
the sinner, the repentant sinner.
Let the sword flash,
let the blood flow,
and the immortal palm
awaits you in heaven!
(1st 4 lines are repeated)
God wills it, God ordains it,
Spare no one!
(various lines are repeated)

SAINT-BRIS

Silence, my friends!

FIRST MONK
Silence, mes amis!

SAINT-BRIS
Que rien ne nous trahisse!

FIRST MONK
Que rien ne nous trahisse!

SAINT-BRIS and FIRST MONK
Retirons-nous sans bruit!

ALL OTHERS
Pour cette cause sainte
SAINT-BRIS, MONK, CHORUS
J'obéirai sans crainte, (line is repeated)

A mon Dieu, à mon Dieu, à mon roi!
Comptez sur mon courage;
Entre vos mains j'engage, (line is
    repeated)
Mes serments, mes serments et ma foi!

FIRST MONK
Silence, my friends!

SAINT-BRIS
Let nothing betray us!

FIRST MONK
Let nothing betray us!

SAINT-BRIS and FIRST MONK
Withdraw without noise!

ALL OTHERS
For this holy cause
SAINT-BRIS, MONK, CHORUS
I will obey without fear, (line is
    repeated)
for my God, for my God, for my king!
Rely on my courage;
Into your hands I place, (line is
    repeated)
My oaths, my vows and my faith!

Together

SOME IN CHORUS SING:
Que rien ne nous trahisse
Et que de leur supplice
Rien ne les avertisse!
Retirons-nous!

OTHERS IN CHORUS SING:
À minuit! Point de bruit!

ALL
Dieu veut! Oui!

BASSES
À minuit!

Together

SOME IN CHORUS SING:
Let nothing betray us
and let nothing warn them
of their agony!
Withdraw!

At midnight! No noise!

ALL
God wills! Yes!

BASSES
At midnight!

(After all of the men have left the stage, Raoul comes out from behind the tapestry; Valentine comes out of her room; they sing the Grand Duo.)

(They begin to leave, slowly.)

FIRST MONK
À minuit!

OTHERS
À minuit!

FIRST MONK
Point de bruit!

OTHERS
Point de bruit!

FIRST MONK
At midnight!

OTHERS
At midnight!

FIRST MONK
No noise!

OTHERS
No noise!

191. SYMPHONIE FANTASTIQUE, mvt. 5
Songe d'une Nuit du Sabbat
Hector Berlioz (1808-1869)

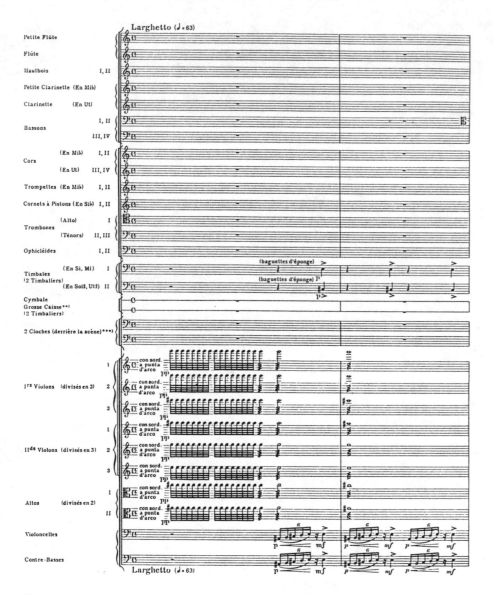

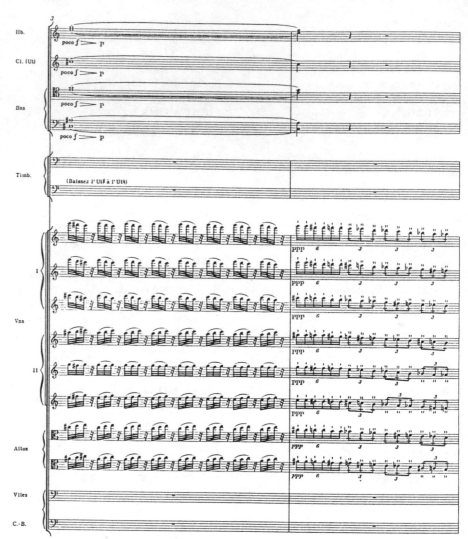

) Placed upright and used as timbale. The second and third timbaliers have sponge beaters. **(HB)

***) If one cannot find 2 bells deep enough for the C and the G written, it is better to use several pianos on the proscenium. They will perform the bell part in double octaves, as written. (HB)

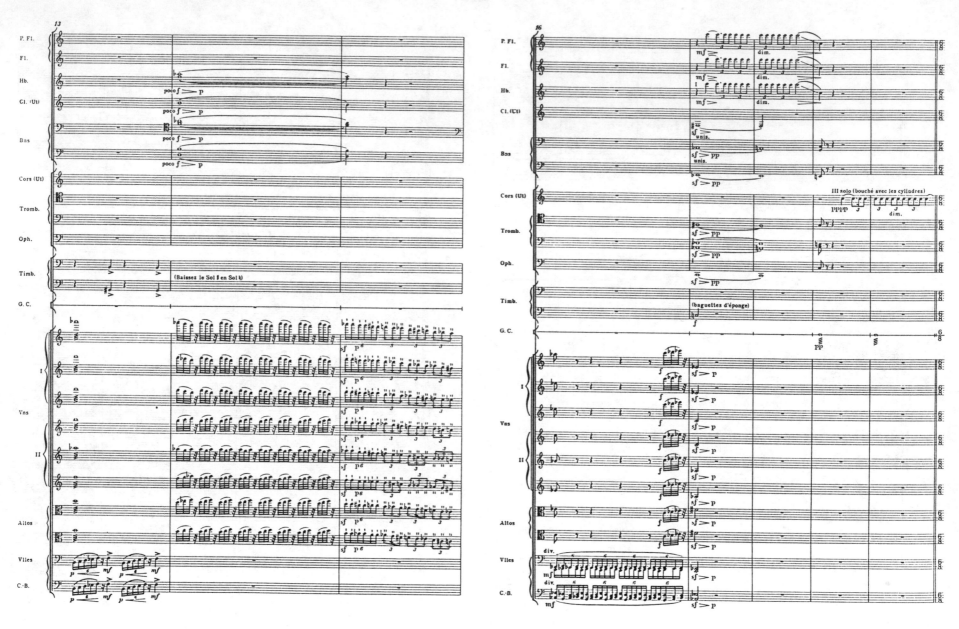

Dies Irae

Ronde du Sabbat

Dies Irae et Ronde du Sabbat ensemble

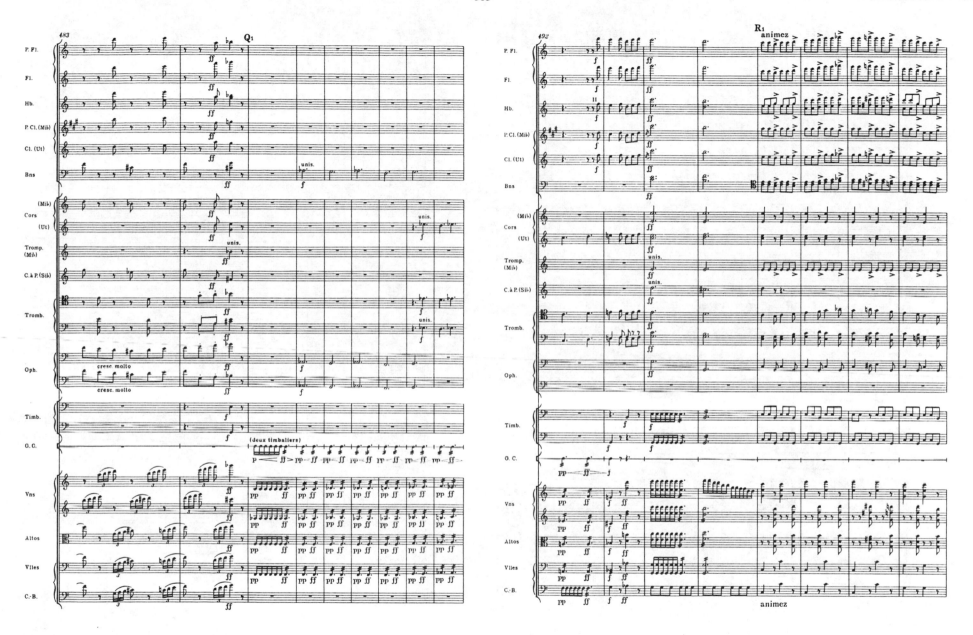

192. NORMA, Act II, Scene 4, Scena e Cavatina: "Casta diva"
Vincenzo Bellini (1801-1835)

Source: Ricordi G. & Company, LTD., Milan

389

Cut to next page (m. 161)

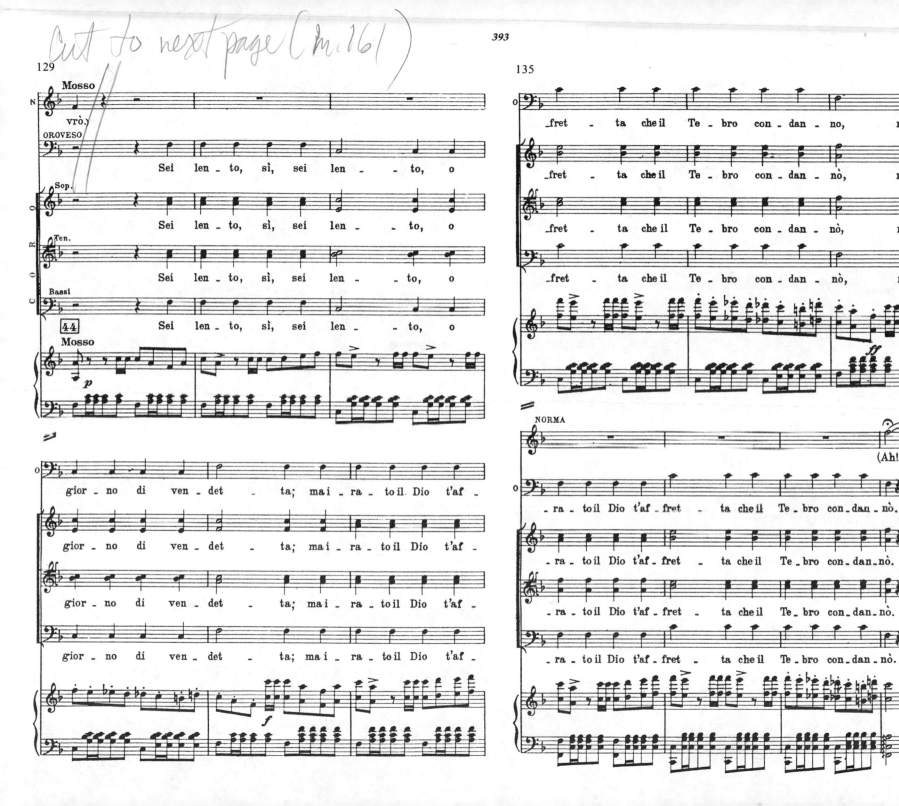

NORMA:

Casta diva, che inargenti
queste sacre antiche piante,
a noi volgi il bel sembiante,
senza nube e senza vel.

(Stanza is repeated by Oroveso and Chorus)

NORMA (joined by Oroveso and Chorus):

Tempra, o Diva, tu de' cori ardenti,

tempra ancora lo zelo audace,
spargi in terra, ah, quella pace
che regnar tu fai nel ciel.

NORMA:

Fine al rito; e il sacro bosco

sia disgombro dia profani.
Quando il Nume irato e fosco
chiegga il sangue dei Romani,
dal druidico delubro
la mia voce tuonerà.

OROVESO and Chorus:

Tuoni, e un sol del popol empio

non isfugga al giusto scempio;
e premier da noi percosso
il Proconsole cadrà.

NORMA:

Cadrà . . . punirlo io posso . . .
(Ma punirlo il cor non sa.)

(Ah! bello a me ritorna
del fido amor primiero:
e contro il mondo intiero
difensa a te sarò.

NORMA:

Chaste goddess, who silvers
these sacred ancient plants,
turn your lovely gaze on us,
unclouded and unveiled.

NORMA (joined by Oroveso and Chorus):

Temper, o goddess, you of the ardent
    hearts,
temper more the bold zeal,
diffuse on earth, ah, that peace
that you make reign in heaven.

NORMA:

The rite is finished; and let the sacred
    woods
be cleared of laymen. [or, profane ones]
When the angry and gloomy god
demands the blood of the Romans,
from the druid shrine
my voice will thunder forth.

OROVESO and Chorus:

Let it thunder forth, and let not one of
    the
impious people escape the just slaughter;
and at the first of our blows
the Proconsul will fall.

NORMA:

He will fall . . . I can punish him . . .
(But [my] heart doesn't know how to
    punish him.)
(Ah! love, return to me
the faithful first love:
and against the entire world
your defense I will be.

Ah! bello a me ritorna
del raggio tuo sereno;
e vita nel tuo seno
e patria e cielo avrò.)

OROVESO and Chorus:

Sei lento, sì, sei lento,
o giorno di vendetta;
ma irato il Dio t'affretta
che il Tebro condannò.

NORMA sings again the text "Ah! bello a me ritorna . . ." to end of stanza.

OROVESO and Chorus sing text from "ma irato, . . ." to end of that stanza.

NORMA:

(Ah! riedi ancora
qual eri allora,
quando, ah, quando il cor
ti diedi allora,
qual eri allora,
quando, ah, quando il cor ti diedi.
ah, riedi a me.)

As NORMA sings last 3 lines above, OROVESO and Chorus sing:

O giorno, il Dio t'affretta
che il Tebro condannò.

Ah! love, return to me
your serene ray [= gaze];
and life in your bosom
and [both] a native land and heaven I
    will have.)

OROVESO and Chorus:

You are slow, yes, you are slow,
oh day of revenge;
but the angry god hurries you
whom the Tiber condemned.

NORMA:

(Ah! return again
to what you were then,
when, ah, when my heart
I gave to you then,
as you were then,
when, ah, when I gave you my heart.
ah, return to me.)

O day, the god hastens you
whom the Tiber condemned.

—Felice Romani

Appendix A: Names of Instruments and Abbreviations

This table sets forth the English, Italian, German, and French names used in music scores for the various musical instruments, together with their respective abbreviations. Presentation is in the arrangement that has become standard in instrumental scores, reading from the top of the score down: Woodwinds, Brass, Percussion, Strings. Those instruments that are used only occasionally are presented last in this table.

Woodwinds

English	Italian	German	French
Piccolo (Picc.)	Flauto piccolo (Fl. Picc.)	Kleine Flöte (Kl. Fl.)	Petite flûte; Flûte piccolo (Fl. picc.)
Flute (Fl.)	Flauto (Fl.); Flauto grande (Fl. gr.)	Grosse Flöte (Fl. gr.)	Flûte (Fl.)
Alto Flute	Flauto contralto (Fl. c-alto)	Altflöte	Flûte en sol
	[pl., Flauti]	[pl., Flöten]	[pl., Flûtes]
Oboe (Ob.)	Oboe (Ob.)	Hoboe (Hb.); Oboe (Ob.)	Hautbois (Hb.)
	[pl., Oboi]	[pl., Hoboen, Oboen]	[pl., Hautbois]
English Horn (E. H.)	Corno inglese (C.; C.i.; Cor. ingl.)	Englisches Horn (Englh.; E. H.)	Cor anglais (C. A.)
Sopranino Clarinet	Clarinetto piccolo (Cl. picc.; Clar. picc.)		
Clarinet (C.; Cl.; Clt.; Clar.)	Clarinetto (Cl.; Clar.)	Klarinette (Kl.)	Clarinette (Cl.)
	[pl., Clarinetti]	[pl., Klarinetten]	[pl., Clarinettes]
Bass Clarinet (B. Cl.)	Clarinetto basso (Cl. b.; Cl. basso; Clar. basso)	Bassklarinette (Bkl.; Bs. Kl.; B.-Kl.)	Clarinette basse (Cl. bs.)
Bassoon (Bsn.; Bssn.)	Fagotto (Fag.; Fg.)	Fagott (Fag.; Fg.)	Basson (Bssn.)
Contrabassoon (C. Bsn.)	Contrafagotto (Cfg.; C. Fag.; Cont. F.)	Kontrafagott (Kfg.)	Contrebasson (C. bssn.; Cbn.)
	[pl., Fagotti]	[pl., Fagotte]	[pl., Bassons]

Brass

English	Italian	German	French
French Horn, or Horn (Hr.; Hn.)	Corno (Cor.; C.)	Horn (Hr.)	Cor; Cor à piston
	[pl., Corni]	[pl., Hörner (Hrn.)]	[pl., Cors]
Trumpet (Tpt.; Trpt.; Trp.; Tr.)	Tromba (Tr.)	Trompete (Tr.; Trp.)	Trompette (Tr.)
	[pl., Trombe]	[pl., Trompeten]	[pl., Trompettes]
Trombone (Tr.; Tbe.; Trb.; Trbe.; Trm.)	Trombone (Tbn.)	Posaune (Ps.; Pos.)	Trombone (Trb.)
	[pl., Tromboni (Tbni.; Trni.)]	[pl., Posaunen]	[pl., Trombones]
Tuba (Tb.)	Tuba (Tb.; Tba.)	Tuba (Tb.); Basstuba (Btb.)	Tuba (Tb.)

Percussion

English	Italian	German	French
Percussion (Perc.)	Percussione	Schlagzeug (Schlag.)	Batterie (Batt.)
Timpani (Timp.); Kettledrums (K. D.)	Timpani (Timp.; Tp.)	Pauken (Pk.)	Timbales (Timb.)
Snare Drum (S. D.)	Tamburo piccolo (Tamb. picc.); Tamburo militaire	Kleine Trommel (Kl. Tr.)	Caisse Claire (C. cl.); Tambour (Militaire) (Tamb. milit.)
Tenor Drum (T. Dr.)	Cassa Rullante	Wirbeltrommel	Caisse Roulante
Bass Drum (B. Dr.)	Gran Cassa (G. C.; Gr. C.; Gr. Cassa)	Grosse Trommel (Gr. Tr.)	Grosse Caisse (Gr. c.)
Cymbals (Cym.; Cymb.)	Piatti (P.; Ptti.; Piat.)	Becken (Beck.)	Cymbales (Cym.)
Tambourine (Tamb.)	Tamburino (Tamb.)	Schellentrommel; Tambourin (Tamb.)	Tambour de Basque (T. de B.; Tamb. de B.; Tamb. de Basque)
Triangle (Trgl.)	Triangolo (Trgl.)	Triangel	Triangle (Triang.)
Tam-tam; Gong (Tam-T.)	Tam-tam	Tam-tam	Tam-tam
Orchestra Bells; Glockenspiel (Glsp.)	Campanelli (Cmp.)	Glockenspiel (Glsp.)	Jeu de Timbres; Carillon
Tubular Bells; Chimes	Campane (Cmp.)	Glocken	Jeu de Cloches; Cloches
Antique Cymbals; Crotales (Crot.)	Piatti antichi; Crotali	Zimbeln; Antiken Zimbeln	Cymbales Antiques; Crotales
Xylophone (Xyl.)	Xilofono	Xylophon	Xylophone (Xyl.)
Siren			Sirène
Cowbells	Cencerro	Kuhlglocken; Herdenglocken	Sonnailles
Wood Blocks (W. Bl.)	Blocco de Legno Cinese	Holzblock	Bloc de Bois
Castanets	Castagnette	Kastagnetten	Castagnettes

Strings

English	Italian	German	French
Violin (V.; Vln.; Vi.)	Violino (V.; Vl.; Vln.)	Violine (V.; Vl.; Vln.) Geige (Gg.)	Violon (V.; Vl.; Vln.)
Viola (Va.; Vl.) [pl., Vas.]	Viola (Va.; Vla.) [pl., Viole (Vle.)]	Bratsche (Br.)	Alto (A.)
Violoncello; 'Cello (Vcl.; Vc.)	Violoncello (Vc.; Vlc.; Vcllo.)	Violoncell (Vc.; Vlc.)	Violoncelle (Vc.)
Double Bass (D. Bs.)	Contrabasso (Cb.; C.B.) [pl., Contrabassi; Bassi (C. Bassi; Bi.)]	Kontrabass (Kb.)	Contrebasse (C.-B.)

Other Instruments Used Occasionally

When included in the orchestra, notation for these instruments is usually placed in the score between percussion and strings.

English	Italian	German	French
Harp (Hp.; Hrp.)	Arpa (A.; Arp.)	Harfe (Hrf.)	Harpe (Hp.)
Piano (Pno.)	Pianoforte (P-f.; Pft.)	Klavier (Kl.)	Piano
Celeste (Cel.)	Celesta	Celesta	Célesta
Harpsichord	Cembalo	Cembalo	Clavecin
Organ (Org.)	Organo	Orgel	Orgue

Appendix B: Some Technical Terms
Frequently Used in Orchestral Scores

English	Italian	German	French
Muted; With mute(s)	Con sordino	mit Dämpfer; Gedämpft (for horns)	Sourdine(s)
Take off mutes	Via sordini	Dämpfer(n) Weg	Enlevez les sourdines
Without mute	Senza sordino	Ohne Dämpfer	Sans sourdine
Divided	Divisi (div.)	Geteilt (get.)	Divisé(e)s (div.)
Divided in 3 parts (or whatever number is specified)	div. a 3	Dreifach	div. à 3
In unison (unis.)	Unisono (unis.)	Zusammen	Unis
Solo	Solo	Allein	Seul
All	Tutti	Alle	Tous
(First player only) 1.	1°	1ste; einfach	1er
1., 2. (first and second players on separate parts)	1°, 2°	1ste, 2te	1er, 2e
a2 (2 players on same part)	a2	zu 2	à 2
Near the bridge	Sul ponticello	am Steg	Sur le chevalet
Bow over the fingerboard	Sul tastiera; Sul tasto	am Griffbrett	sur la touche
With the wood of the bow	Col legno	mit Holz; col Legno	Avec le bois
At the point of the bow	Punta d'arco	Spitze	Pointe; de la pointe
At the frog of the bow	al Tallone	am Frosch	du talon
Half (half of a string section is to play)	la metà	die Hälfte	la moitié
Stopped (horns)	Chiuso; chiusi	Gestopft	Bouché; bouchés
Open	Aperto; aperti	Offen	Ouvert
With soft stick; with soft mallet	Bacchetta di spugna	mit Schwammschlegel	Baguette d'éponge; baguette molle
With hard stick(s)	Bacchette di legno	mit Holzschlegeln	Baguette(s) en bois
(Directive to change tuning, or instrument):			
Change C to E	Sol Muta in Mi	C nach E umstimmen	Changez Do en Mi
Change to piccolo (or whatever instr.)	Muta in Piccolo	Piccolo nehmen	Changez en piccolo
Stand, or Desk	Leggio	Pult	Pupitre
Ordinary; In ordinary way (play in ordinary manner, after having played sul ponticello, for example)	Modo ordinario	Gewöhnlich	Mode ordinaire; position nat.

Index